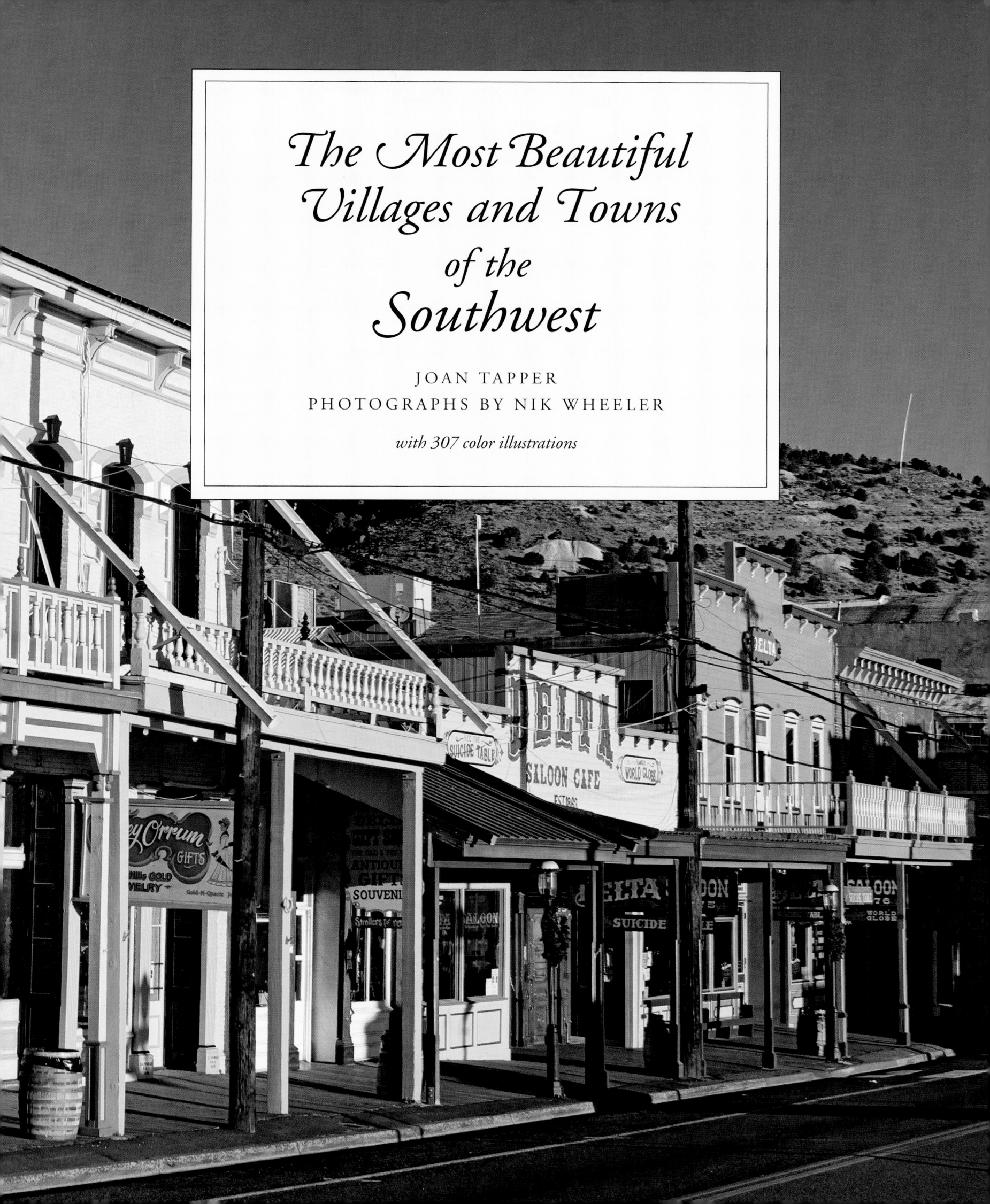

The Most Beautiful
Villages and Towns
of the
Southwest

JOAN TAPPER

PHOTOGRAPHS BY NIK WHEELER

with 307 color illustrations

HALF TITLE PAGE: *A* ristra *of drying red chilis brightens an antique store façade in Tubac, Arizona*

TITLE PAGES: *"C" Street, Virginia City, Nevada*

OPPOSITE: *A thirst-quenching establishment in Jerome, Arizona* (top)*; sign for the Apache Motel in Moab, Utah* (center)*; spicy wall decorations at La Hacienda de Los Martinez in Taos, New Mexico* (bottom)

Designed by Liz Rudderham

Copyright © 2009 Thames & Hudson Ltd, London
Text © 2009 Joan Tapper
Photographs © 2009 Nik Wheeler

First published in 2009 in hardcover in the United States of America by Thames & Hudson Inc., 500 Fifth Avenue, New York, New York 10110

thamesandhudsonusa.com

Library of Congress Catalog Card Number 2009900934

ISBN 978-0-500-51468-9

Printed and bound in Singapore by C.S. Graphics

Contents

Introduction

Think of the American Southwest, and it isn't the towns that first come to mind but the incredible landscape. The carved-out chasms, jagged heights, and dramatic desert expanses are what stand out, whether you're looking down from an airplane or driving cross-country.

But you shouldn't miss the beautiful old towns — the clusters of adobe houses around Spanish-style plazas, and the rows of Victorian miners' cottages that still cling to precipitous hillsides. Many of these communities started as remote, inhospitable outposts, then flourished in a burst of riches, only to fade again. Today they are blossoming once more: the Southwest is a region of energetic growth and multicultural vitality, and its quaint towns are enjoying renewed attention

The Southwest is an immense area, taking in Arizona, Nevada, New Mexico, Utah, and western Colorado, about 1,000 miles from east to west and 750 miles from north to south, roughly half a million square miles in all. Its geophysical wonders are the showpieces of 16 national parks and many more national monuments, to say nothing of its many national historical parks and trails. The mountains are dazzling – Colorado alone has 53 peaks that tower above 14,000 feet – while the canyons carved by eons of river water are magnificent. There's a lot to marvel at.

This vast and diverse region is united by a shared history. Virtually all of the Southwest was once Spanish Territory, the part of the American frontier lying west of the Louisiana Purchase and south of Oregon Country. (California and Texas belonged to the same territory, but California has its own unique history – and its own book of *Most Beautiful Villages and Towns* – while the vast Lone Star State also followed an idiosyncratic path.) Spain claimed all this land in the 1500s, and Francisco Vásquez de Coronado trekked up into Colorado and beyond as he searched for the fabled gold of Quivira, but after he found none, the Spanish concentrated their efforts in Arizona and New Mexico. Santa Fe remained on the far frontier of New Spain, and the land was populated mostly by Native Americans, including the Hopi and Pueblo tribes, Navajos and Apaches, the O'odham, Utes, and Paiutes.

Things began to change with Mexican independence in 1821. Mountain men and trappers explored the region, swapping stories and

Symbols of history, religious heritage, and cuisine make a striking display at a New Mexico shop (opposite). *Throughout the Southwest, currents of several cultures have contributed to towns and villages with enduring appeal.* Below: *The Victorian-style St. James Hotel in Cimarron, New Mexico, invites contemporary visitors to wind down to a 19th-century pace.*

The effects of wind and water on sandstone created the formations of Arches National Park in Utah, where half of Double Arch (far left) suggests an eye on the cloudless sky. The state is rife with wildly scenic areas in which the national bird (left) can keep its own eagle eye out for prey.

information that later would be incorporated into wagon routes. As traders opened the Santa Fe Trail, new towns sprang up along the way. When the Mexican–American War ended in 1848, the concluding treaty ceded almost all of the Southwest to the United States; the Gadsden Purchase five years later added the last swath of land along the southern border.

This acquisition was huge, but not particularly desirable, at least not to ordinary settlers. The climate was extreme – too cold in mountain winters, too hot in summer at lower elevations. Short growing seasons and lack of rainfall promised little to farmers, and the area was still the homeland of Indian tribes whose raids and attacks were deservedly feared.

When California's siren call of gold went out to the world in 1848, the fortune seekers crossing the continent headed straight for the mining camps with barely a glance at the land they traversed. Only one group of pioneers found in the Great Basin the sanctuary they craved. In 1847, Brigham Young – successor to Joseph Smith, the founder of the Church of Latter Day Saints (or Mormons) – led the first group of believers to the banks of the Great Salt Lake. Over the next decades thousands more Mormon settlers followed, and Young dispatched hundreds of them in well-organized parties to colonize the territory he called Deseret.

Eventually, as the gold prospectors in California gave up on their prospects, they took a second look at the mountains to the east. Indeed there was gold... and silver, copper, lead, and zinc – enough to set off wave after wave of frenzied mining, creating boomtowns (and ghost towns) by the dozens. By the 1860s, the new mineral wealth had attracted the attention of the U.S. Government, which needed money to fund the Civil War. Looking to benefit from Virginia City's mines, Congress quickly carved a separate Nevada Territory out of Utah, and granted it statehood in 1864. Arizona Territory was split off from New Mexico, placing its capital out of the reach of Confederate sympathizers. After the Civil War ended, the forts that had been set up as Union outposts found themselves protecting burgeoning towns and new transportation lines, and, now that the tide of settlement was turning, removing Native Americans from their homelands.

In the last decades of the 19th century, energy and innovation helped to unite the Southwest to the rest of the country. The Golden Spike completed the transcontinental railroad in 1869, and soon afterward spur lines and narrow-gauge tracks were threading through the mountains to link remote mines to mills, smelters, and markets. Engineering skills helped keep Southwestern towns alive, as technological developments periodically were able to make unproductive mineshafts lucrative again.

In the end, though, the residents of mining towns saw their livelihoods disappear, and by the 1930s communities that owed their prosperity to rail lines also suffered badly. Virtually every town and village in this book had "quiet years" that in some cases almost did them in.

The bad times, however, ultimately proved a blessing. Though old houses occasionally were moved or even burned for fuel, a general lack of funds kept historic structures standing. In some cases it was hippies who rediscovered these places; elsewhere it was preservationists or entrepreneurial visionaries. Within these small communities, passionate local advocates worked to create historic districts, found regional museums, and preserve their heritage. As a result of their efforts, many small Southwestern towns have experienced a renaissance over the past few decades.

The places in this book range from tiny villages of a few hundred people to towns of as much as 40,000, but most are the kind of place where a chance conversation still opens doors. In Trinidad, Colorado, for instance, a few questions led to the one-time newspaper publisher, who had the keys to a closed museum. In Spring City, a chance encounter in a café resulted in invitations to several beautifully restored homes. History buffs turned up everywhere: the owner of a bed-and-breakfast inn in Virginia City, a house painter in Las Vegas who specialized in Victorian

*W*estern traditions live on in Steamboat Springs, Colorado (above left), where ranchers drive cattle down the main street as part of July 4th celebrations. From a tufted settee in the bar of Telluride's New Sheridan Hotel (above) the streetscape outside looks largely unchanged – except for clothing styles – since the building went up in 1895.

An unexpected vision of Nevada persists in the agricultural settlement of Paradise Valley (opposite) near Winnemucca. Similar surprises await in Genoa, whose gingerbread-trimmed Pink House (above) was built by the Mormon station's founder, John Reese, in 1853.

mansions, and a former TV reporter in Park City, to name a few. They all were eager to pass along interesting stories and local lore.

In such an incredible region, it was hard to narrow down our choices, but Nik Wheeler and I finally settled on 28 communities to represent the Southwest's vivid history and variety. Chimayó, Truchas, and Las Trampas, Mesilla, and Tubac and Tumacácori, for example, all date back to early Spanish settlements. Tombstone and Virginia City are colorful settings associated with legendary Western characters and events.

Most places in this book are treasure troves of late-19th-century architecture, reflecting Victorian building sprees usually based on mining prosperity, railway wealth, or a combination of both. In Arizona, such 19th-century boomtowns include Bisbee and Jerome, as well as Prescott, which was a territorial capital. In New Mexico, there's Las Vegas, Raton, and Cimarron; Colorado boasts Aspen, Breckenridge, Durango and Silverton, Georgetown and Idaho Springs, Ouray, Telluride, and Trinidad. Some of these towns, like Park City in Utah, have capitalized on their old-fashioned atmosphere even as they've developed into major ski resorts.

The rich and diverse cultural heritage of the Southwest contributes to the distinctive character of its communities. Steamboat Springs, another Colorado ski mecca, draws on its ranching history, while in Nevada, Basque immigrants have given the crossroads town of Winnemucca a memorable flavor. Genoa, Manti, Spring City, and Ephraim exemplify the heritage of their Mormon founders. Taos combines Native American, Hispanic, and Anglo influences, while Sedona has developed as a New Age center surrounded by spectacular red rocks.

Finally, several of these towns are gateways to awe-inspiring parklands. Boulder and Escalante, Bluff, Kanab, and Moab offer convenient starting points for explorations in the Grand Canyon, Bryce and Zion Canyons, Capitol Reef, Canyonlands, Arches, Grand Staircase-Escalante, and Lake Powell, as well as unforgettable trips on the Colorado, Green, and San Juan rivers.

Interspersed with the chapters are four photographic essays that touch on broader themes: the landscape and the movies, historic Route 66, ghost towns, and ancient and contemporary Native American life.

The sound of a saw once summoned worshipers to the 1880 Congregational church in Silverton (top). *Skiers heed the call of the Southwest's spectacular snowfields* (above).

If the towns and villages in these pages have come out at the positive end of rags-to-riches-to-rags-to-riches sagas, they still face 21st-century challenges: real-estate frenzies that threaten to exclude longtime residents, increased traffic, environmental concerns, and the need to keep a well-rooted community from evolving into an impersonal resort. Each of these places confronts those issues in its own, sometimes quite innovative, way.

It is ironic that towns once so difficult to live in are now among the most desirable destinations in our lifestyle-oriented age. The desert communities have blossomed with golf courses and retirement homes. The snow-covered slopes are skiers' delights. In summer, old rocky paths over dizzying mountain passes turn into exhilarating biking or hiking trails. River rafting, off-road riding, rock-climbing, and other sports draw 20- and 30-somethings not only to vacation but also to move in permanently. And the inspirational qualities of these spectacular mesas and buttes attract artists and New Agers who are energized by their power.

For the beautiful villages and towns of the Southwest, these are boom times indeed, thanks to our quest for physical and spiritual well-being – contemporary riches as alluring as silver or gold.

Arizona

Bisbee

BEFORE YOU EMBARK on a Queen Mine tour, they put a hard hat on your head and a yellow slicker over your clothes. An unexpectedly heavy battery pack is strapped around your waist – to fuel a light while you're underground. Duly outfitted, you board a narrow tram for a close-up glimpse of the copper-mining industry that gave birth to Bisbee and sustained it for a century.

As you travel horizontally into the heart of the mountain – 700 feet, then 1,500 feet – your guide, a former miner, takes you back in time. He explains how mules first pulled the ore cars and points out the timbers that shored up tunnels and cave-like stopes, where the miners worked. Finally he demonstrates how the miners set dynamite charges to loosen the rock and pull out the ore deposits. That kind of tough, exhausting work extracted 8 billion pounds of copper from the area between 1877 and 1975. And it built the town, whose pretty turn-of-the-century architecture still clings to Bisbee's steep hillsides.

The first prospectors arrived in 1878, setting up their tents in a place called Mule Gulch. Two years later, army scouts found silver deposits in the area, but copper proved more prevalent. To extract it, companies needed well-heeled financiers to bankroll the construction of mines and smelters. By 1880, the Phelps Dodge Mining Company had organized the Copper Queen Consolidated Mining Company, and Mule Gulch acquired a new name – Bisbee – to honor a major investor.

Bisbee grew quickly, prospering with the development of new technologies, like electric power, which required the use of copper wire. By 1910 there were 29,000 people jammed into the town, and the mines worked round the clock. So did the businesses that sustained the miners, an international crowd from places like Cornwall, Armenia, Croatia, Serbia, Wales, and Italy. Saloons and houses of ill repute lined the infamous road known as Brewery Gulch. There were also churches of every denomination, fraternal organizations,

Bisbee's well-preserved downtown (above) is shadowed by the Mule Mountains that are bristled by prickly pear cactus (opposite) but laced by rich veins of copper. At the town's peak, 29,000 people lived and worked here, keeping mines busy 24 hours a day. Now the Queen Mine opens its underground shafts (left) only for properly suited-up visitors on tour. Page 13: Sedona's red rock buttes capture the imagination of artists and ordinary travelers alike.

a women's club, a posh hotel, and three opera houses. These manifestations of civic and commercial pride rose along narrow streets that branched off on different levels connected by sets of stairs. Many buildings have endured; 240 properties are included in a historic district that displays architectural styles from the 1890s to the 1930s, though the uses of the buildings may have changed. The imposing 1897 Copper Queen company offices have been turned into the Bisbee Mining & Historical Museum. Steps away is the Copper Queen Hotel, an Italianate structure that first welcomed mining executives and investors in 1902.

The Renaissance-style Muheim Block, at the corner of Brewery Avenue, began as a saloon in 1905 but later housed Arizona's first stock exchange. The columned Bank of Bisbee remains a bank, while the Pythian Castle, built in 1904 for the fraternal order of the Knights of Pythias, rises above the townscape with a graceful Renaissance Revival clock tower.

Mining accounted for the largest part of the payroll, with early miners earning between $3.50 and $4.50 a day. In 1917 the radical International Workers of the World (IWW) prevailed on 3,000 men here to strike. As America had recently entered World War I, the

Years of industrious effort left their mark in the terraced cuts at the Lavender Pit mine (opposite). *A lighter artist's touch is evident in a dreamy mural* (above) *on a motel wall.* Left: *Playtime outside the Bisbee Mining & Historical Museum.*

strikers were considered unpatriotic. On July 12, 1917, 2,000 armed citizens rounded up 1,200 union sympathizers, loaded them onto boxcars, and shipped them to New Mexico. The "Bisbee Deportation" provoked national outrage, but from then on, Bisbee was unquestionably a company town, its fortunes tied to the nation's need for copper. Mining declined during the Depression, accelerated with World War II, and was maintained by increasingly efficient methods of extraction until 1975. When the mines finally closed, it looked like Bisbee, too, would be shuttered.

Instead, the low cost of real estate and the appealing setting attracted artists, hippies, and later a few retirees, who gave the town a new colorful persona. They filled the historic buildings with antique malls, art and sculpture galleries, pottery studios, and boutiques. A quirky array of structures – including the old city hall, a former jail, a schoolhouse, and a collection of vintage travel trailers – have been turned into offbeat and appealing accommodations.

Meanwhile the town embraces its heritage with an unconventional "scenic" viewpoint. At the edge of town you can ponder the overwhelming concavity of the open Lavender Pit mine, three-quarters of a mile wide, a mile and a quarter long, 950 feet deep. It's all that's left of a copper-rich hill, a stunning testament to the ability of men to move mountains.

A lofty backdrop to a mine relic on the museum grounds, the Presbyterian Church (opposite) has been a Bisbee fixture since 1903. Artifacts from mid-century, the retro trailers at The Shady Dell (below) have found a new use as lodgings for travelers, who may choose to top things off with the offerings at Optimo Custom Hatworks (left).

*H*aving survived its ghost town era, Jerome once again enjoys its moment in the sun (above). The huge 1927 Spanish Mission-style hospital, now a hotel, stands at the top of the road that zigzags upward past turn-of-the-century houses and shops (left) recently taken up by artists.

Jerome

As YOU DRIVE the switchback road twisting its way up to Jerome, the old mining town appears to have only a precarious hold on the summit of Cleopatra Hill. In this case looks are not deceiving. Jerome officially hit ghost-town status in the 1950s, with just 50 residents. But it stubbornly held on, and today, with a population almost ten times that number, Jerome's precipitous streets and turn-of-the-century buildings are engaging relics of a memorable boom-and-bust saga.

Everyone came here seeking ore, beginning with the Native Americans who dug mines 1,000 years ago to get azurite and other minerals that could be used for body paint. Spanish explorers passed through in a futile search for gold. Then in 1876 an Army scout filed a mining claim for copper. He was quickly followed by other prospectors. But before long, the miners had sold their diggings to eastern financiers who could afford to develop the claims. By 1883 the United Verde Copper Company had been formed with long-distance investors who included Eugene Jerome – a cousin of Jennie Jerome, Winston Churchill's mother. Jerome refused to put up any money unless the haphazard camp of tents and shacks was named for him, and so it was. The new mine prospered as long as the price of copper was high. When the price plunged in 1884, however, United Verde shut down.

The tales of those early days, along with tools, artifacts, and assorted memorabilia, form part of the exhibits in the local historical society's Mine Museum on Main Street. The museum also profiles Jerome's major figures, among them Senator William Clark of Montana, who was so impressed with a sample of Jerome's ore that he bought United Verde in 1888 and turned it into the richest privately owned copper mine in the world.

In 1900 Jerome was the fourth-largest town in the Arizona Territory, with 2,861 people and a reputation for wicked ways. Bars and bordellos abounded, accounting for the nickname Husband's Alley, where ladies of easy virtue plied their trade. The town's makeshift wooden buildings burned again and again, until most had been rebuilt with fireproof brick.

Meanwhile, a second mine, the Little Daisy, had opened nearby. In 1912 James "Rawhide" Douglas bought the enterprise and moved to town. Within four years he had built an adobe-brick mansion – now a state historic park – overlooking the mine, with fine accoutrements like a wine cellar, marble shower, and a central vacuum system, which he showed off to the mine officials and investors who were his frequent guests.

Jerome's underground shafts were eventually supplemented by an open pit mine – Arizona's first – but the network of tunnels had an unforeseen effect. In the 1920s, as the town's population was peaking at 15,000, the streets began to collapse, causing buildings to slide down the hillside. The jail, for example, actually moved 225 feet across the road before foundations could be stabilized.

*O*ld cars and trucks have a resting place on the sprawling premises of the Gold King Mine (opposite) *just outside Jerome. Visitors to town can lay their head at the Hotel Connor* (left), *which first rented rooms – $1 a night – in 1898. Accommodations at the House of Joy* (above) *originally came with female company. Today the sign denotes a boutique.*

*M*ine cars line up at Jerome
State Historic Park (left),
empty except of memories, like those
passed on by Gold King Mine
proprietor Don Robertson (above).

The Depression closed the mines until 1935, when the Phelps Dodge Mining Company, which ran the copper operations in Bisbee, stepped in and again put men to work. World War II ensured that the miners were busy throughout the 1940s. Then in 1953, PD, as the company was known, shut down production for good. Without jobs, the workers left, and PD began moving buildings out of town.

But that wasn't the end. The few dozen residents who stayed embraced Jerome's "ghost town" designation and convinced PD to leave whatever structures remained. A decade later those empty spaces proved attractive to the artists who set up studios and created Jerome's new countercultural reputation. In 1966 the town was declared a National Historic District.

Today Jerome's boarding houses, saloons, residences, and business blocks – even the old town hall – are filled with boutiques, restaurants, bed-and-breakfasts, and lodgings. The hospital, which was built in 1927, has been transformed into a hilltop hotel. The old Liberty Theater displays movie memorabilia and a 1928 organ while the building's owners work to restore the venue to its former glory. And a score of serious art galleries, including many in the converted rooms of the old high school, welcome visitors to a popular art walking tour once a month.

Jerome is an easy place to strike up conversations. Ask residents what brought them there, and they'll talk about the quiet, the affordability, and perhaps the views. Indeed, on a clear winter day, residents and visitors alike pause to stare at a rainbow over the stunning panorama that stretches across the valley, beyond the old mine works, to the snowcapped red rocks of the Mogollon Rim and the tantalizing San Francisco Peaks more than 60 miles away.

*B*uilt to transport copper from Jerome to the smelter at Clarkdale, the Verde Canyon Railroad (above) *now carries passengers on a scenic four-hour journey through mountains laced with malachite, the green ore that suggested the name of the picturesque Verde Valley.*

Prescott

ONCE A MONTH the ladies of Prescott's Victorian Society don hoopskirts and feathered millinery and meet for lunch in a downtown restaurant. If you happen to see them waiting to cross the street by the plaza, they don't seem particularly out of place. There's a turn-of-the-century gentility here, accentuated by the solid brick and stone edifices that surround the stately columned courthouse.

The place wasn't always so proper, of course. Montezuma Street, along the west side of the plaza, was named "Whiskey Row" for a reason. With 26 saloons in 24 building sites, there were plenty of opportunities for a little territorial pandemonium. Chaos reigned supreme on the hot July day in 1900 when a fire swept along this street and ten nearby blocks, obliterating the wooden structures of the young community.

Prescott was founded in 1864, a year after President Abraham Lincoln was finally persuaded by discoveries

of gold in the area – and a desire to use it to pay for the Civil War – to split off an Arizona Territory from New Mexico. He dispatched a party led by John Goodwin, the newly appointed territorial governor, to find a place for the capital. Goodwin eventually settled on a pine-shaded site near Granite Creek, close to a miners' camp, and built the Governor's Mansion. The name is grander than the actual structure, which is a rough-walled, single-story log cabin that not only served as residence for both Goodwin and his territorial secretary, Richard McCormick, but was also used as their offices and as an occasional meeting place for the legislature.

Goodwin and McCormick named the new town Prescott in honor of a historian who had made a literary splash with a book that claimed – erroneously – that Aztecs and Toltecs were responsible for ancient Native American cliff dwellings in the region. The actual Indian residents of the area, the Yavapai, were forcibly relocated to the Apache reservation near San Carlos in 1875 and only allowed to return two decades later.

The Governor's Mansion is now the centerpiece of the Sharlot Hall Museum, which comprises half a dozen buildings that tell the story of Prescott's early days. These include Fort Misery, a pioneer's bare-bones cabin built in 1863–64; a replica of the first public schoolhouse; a ranch house that was reconstructed in the 1930s to demonstrate how early settlers lived; the 1875 home of the colorful fifth territorial governor, John C. Fremont, and his stalwart wife, Jesse; and the gracious Victorian dwelling built in 1877 for the merchant William Coles Bashford. Other exhibits depict local pursuits and pleasures, ranging from ranching to Army life, annual rodeos, and frequent musicales.

The museum is named for one of Prescott's singular figures: Sharlot Hall was born in Kansas and came to Arizona in 1882 as a 12-year-old. Independent and strong-minded, she grew up to be a writer, adventurer, and the territorial historian. In 1927 Hall moved into the Governor's Mansion with the intention of preserving it, and it was her collection of memorabilia that became the foundation of the museum.

You'll find dozens of other historic buildings throughout downtown Prescott, especially around the plaza, where they house an inviting mix of galleries,

Solon Borglum's "Rough Rider," in front of the grand Yavapai County Courthouse (opposite top), *memorializes William "Buckey" O'Neill, a Prescott favorite son who perished in the Spanish–American War. The town's territorial era lives on in the period dress of the Victorian Society members* (opposite below), *while the Palace Bar and Restaurant* (above), *rebuilt after the Whiskey Row fire, showcases photos of other local characters, like the Earp brothers who played cards at the Palace, and Little Egypt, who shimmied here in 1910.*

shops, bars, and restaurants. A few structures survived the raging fire of 1900. The old stone firehouse and jail has become the city's visitor center. The J. I. Gardner store was spared; its atmospheric 1890s interior is incorporated into Murphy's Restaurant. And the vault in the Bank of Arizona building was also found intact after the fire, with its contents "warm but negotiable."

The saloons of Whiskey Row, however, were not so fortunate. The Palace Bar and Restaurant, where the Earp brothers and Doc Holliday once played cards, was destroyed, though patrons carried its mirrored back bar out to the plaza and immediately set up shop there. When the Palace was rebuilt in 1901, the elaborate bar went back in, and it's still there, along with a massive turn-of-the-century icebox, a thick-walled safe, photographs and gambling paraphernalia, and several bullet holes in the ceiling from later fracases.

By 1900 Prescott was no longer the territorial capital, having ceded the honor to Tucson in 1867, regained it from 1877 to 1889, and lost it permanently to Phoenix. But its civic spirit never wavered, encouraging the construction of elegant Victorian mansions on

An expression of civic pride, the Hassayampa Inn (opposite) from 1927 was designed by Henry Trost, who added Spanish Colonial touches to the brick architecture favored by city fathers. A brick-and-granite façade distinguishes the Bank of Arizona building (right) on a corner of the plaza, while a statue adds an unmistakable crowning touch to the Elks Opera House down the block. Victorian homes with wraparound verandas and columned entries line the streets of Prescott's gracious residential areas (below).

Mount Vernon Avenue and Pleasant Street, the Elks Opera House in 1905, and the imposing courthouse itself, completed in 1918.

To accommodate the travelers who were beginning to motor through the West, the city fathers decided to build a first-class hotel. They issued stock certificates and commissioned the Hassayampa Inn, a 1927 treasure with a lobby of painted beams, a tiled fireplace, ornate chandeliers, and etched glass. Noted guests, including Will Rogers and General John J. "Blackjack" Pershing, arrived to sample the hospitality, which was stretched a bit thin when Western movie star Tom Mix rode his horse through the salon.

Cowboys and Western imagery remain an important element of Prescott, thanks in part to artist George Phippen. His paintings and bronzes of ranch hands and Indians inspired the Phippen Museum and the annual Western art show that draws thousands of collectors to town every May. During the rest of the year local heritage is simply a part of daily life.

In a scene that begs for a plein air painter, a fisherman waits for a bite at Granite Basin Lake (right). *The bright cottages of McCormick Street* (above) *constitute an informal arts district, while at Watson Lake* (top) *the colors owe everything to nature.*

Sedona

SEDONA'S RED ROCKS send your imagination into overdrive. Terra-cotta-colored buttes, spires, and pinnacles – their fantastic shapes evoke all kinds of images, reflected in names like Steamboat Rock, Coffee Pot, Cockscomb, and Snoopy. Yet the early history of this community was not focused on stone, but on water – the life-giving Oak Creek, which descends through its spectacular canyon south of Flagstaff.

The creek flows year round, a rarity in Arizona, and Native Americans used it to water their small fields of squash, beans, and corn. But in 1876 army troops led by General George Crook moved the last of the local Indians to an Apache reservation at San Carlos. It wasn't long before J. J. Thompson, an Irish immigrant and entrepreneur, claimed squatter's rights to some of the land and built a cabin at what he called Indian Gardens. Over the next few decades, he was joined by half a dozen other families, who carved out farms and orchards below the scenic vermilion cliffs. Their produce and fruit would eventually go to feed the

Twilight enhances the scarlet hues of the movie-set mountains cradling Sedona (left), where ribbons of holiday stars twinkle over a quiet plaza (below).

33

mountaintop mining community of Jerome, roughly 30 miles away.

Among the new settlers were the Schneblys, who arrived in 1901. A year later Theodore Schnebly became the town's postmaster, and when the government rejected his too-lengthy choices for a name for the little village, he called the place Sedona, after his wife.

The stories of all these pioneers are illustrated in the Sedona Heritage Museum, which is located in the wood-and-brick farmhouse built in 1931 by the Jordan family and enlarged over the years. The rambling rooms are filled with their original furniture, from a dresser and cupboard to a cast-iron stove and the town's first telephone.

*B*lending into its Boynton Canyon setting, Enchantment Resort (above) *takes its architectural cues from adobe pueblos. The Mexican-style village of Tlaquepaque* (left and opposite), *originally envisioned as an artists' live-and-work space, is now a place to shop and dine.*

But the museum's most entertaining exhibits showcase Sedona's striking red rocks and their special place in moviemaking history. Zane Gray had used the area as the setting for his novel *Call of the Canyon*, and in 1923, when the author turned his own story into a screenplay for a silent film, Sedona provided the location. That first shoot was interrupted by a raging summer flood, so it was a decade before Hollywood came calling again. But eventually the lure of the landscape proved too strong. From the 1930s to the 1950s Sedona's cliffs and canyons were the backdrop for some 92 Western feature films and TV shows, including classics like *Johnny Guitar* with Joan Crawford, *Broken Arrow* with Jimmy Stewart and Jeff Chandler, and *Angel and the Badman* with John Wayne.

Ranchers and farmers continued to sustain the region's economy in the 20th century, but its beauty

began to draw visual artists, too. Surrealist painter Max Ernst lived and worked here from 1946 to 1953, and there were enough resident painters and sculptors to found an arts organization in 1958. It continues to this day as the Sedona Arts Center, which holds workshops and classes, as well as exhibitions. Dozens of newer galleries have also opened, including several in Tlaquepaque, a charming re-creation of a Mexican village – complete with tiled fountains, plazas, and a picturesque chapel – which was conceived in 1971 as a complex of live-and-work artists' studios.

As it happened, the growth of the arts scene was a lucky development. When Jerome's mines closed in the early 1950s, the market for Sedona's crops disappeared with it. Instead it was an increasing stream of retirees and tourists that kept the town alive.

Or perhaps something more spiritual was responsible for Sedona's continued popularity. Some say that centuries ago Native Americans felt a connection to these magnificent canyons and held sacred ceremonies there. In the 1950s, inspired by the dramatic setting,

Marguerite Staude, a sculptor and frequent visitor to Sedona, had the Chapel of the Holy Cross built into a cliff at the edge of town, incorporating a stunning view into its cruciform architecture.

In the 1980s New Agers identified several places in Sedona as vortexes, hot spots where the earth's natural energy flows inward or outward, making these areas powerful meditation sites. The four best-known vortexes are found at Airport Mesa, Bell Rock, Cathedral Rock, and Boynton Canyon, but believers point to countless others. It's no surprise, then, to encounter numerous spas in Sedona, along with New Age stores and a wide range of healers, intuitives, and therapists who practice everything from acupuncture, massage, and Reiki to sound-healing and aura-cleansing.

It doesn't take a crystal, though, to see the appeal of Sedona's outdoors. On foot, on a mountain bike, or in a four-wheel-drive vehicle, you can follow a trail up, over, or around timeless red rocks that call to mind a submarine, a chimney, or a camel. Whatever you choose to envision, the exhilaration will be unmistakable.

In the setting sun, New Age enthusiasts channel the energy of the earth at one of Sedona's famed vortexes (above). *Craggy Cathedral Rock* (opposite), *rising beyond Oak Creek, is another spot known for its spiritual power.*

Tombstone

The two men frowned under their ten-gallon hats as they took up their positions in the empty street lined by Western-style false-front emporiums. One man, sporting a handlebar mustache, wore a black vest and a holster on his hip. The other had long hair and was cloaked in a tan duster that hid his weapon. "Looking for a gunfight?" the taller one snarled at a passer-by. Then he handed out a flyer advertising a reenacted shootout at the O.K. Corral.

Entering Tombstone today is like entering a Western movie set – which the town has sometimes been – and volunteering to be an extra. The local saga of the Earp brothers and Doc Holliday has inspired countless movies and television shows. With commercial reenactments daily and hobbyists' shows on weekends, costumed gunslingers and saloon girls are everywhere. You're likely to meet a mountain man in buckskins in the local eatery or bump into a "soiled dove" at the pizzeria.

Tombstone's story began years before the Earps rode into town in 1879, and continued after they left in 1882. In the 1860s this was Apache country, a rugged

didn't stick around to see the place prosper. Offered $300,000 for his claims in 1880, he took the money and left.

Other fortune seekers replaced him, and the claims turned into lucrative mines, though as early as 1881 rising water in the shafts threatened the operations. Tombstone's population swelled to almost 15,000 by 1882, as $25 million in silver was removed in just four years. After that, the town's success rose and fell with silver prices, world events, and local disasters. In 1886 fires destroyed the pumps that kept the mines working; an economic depression followed in 1893; eight years later silver's value was up again. In 1909, however, the pumps failed completely, flooding the mines. Boom times were over.

Pictures, artifacts, and memorabilia in the Tombstone Courthouse museum, which fills a stately brick edifice begun in 1882, tell the story of the town's changing fortunes. Here one meets some of the community's most vivid characters, including Nellie Cashman, the "angel of the camps," who cared for miners and ran a restaurant; Sarah Herring Sorin, who went from teaching school to practicing law; and Camillus Sidney, who ran the local photo studio with his wife, Mollie Fly.

It's easy to imagine these memorable figures on the streets of Tombstone, where the buildings look much as they did in the 1870s, though the shops inside may sell souvenirs, art, Western wear, jewelry, and fudge. Several saloons still pour drinks, of course, like Big Nose Kate's

S hades of the Wild West hover over Allen Street in Tombstone (left), *where even a welcome sign* (opposite) *hints at a turbulent past. On Boot Hill* (below) *restored markers note the resting places of the McLaury brothers and Billy Clanton, who died in the town's most famous incident.*

land of inhospitable hills raided first by the legendary Apache leader Cochise – until he struck a truce in 1872 – and later by Geronimo. It was only after most of the tribe had been relocated to the San Carlos Reservation that the prospectors moved in.

Ed Schieffelin arrived in 1877, ignoring the warning that he'd find nothing in the rocks but his tombstone. He used the name for his first claim and a year later found a rich silver lode. By 1879, the town of Tombstone had sprung up as a haphazard collection of board-and-batten shacks with canvas roofs. Schieffelin

*N*ow a low-key museum, the Tombstone Epitaph *building* (above) *housed the newspaper founded by John Clum in 1880. As the paper's editor he defended the Earps, whose famous Gunfight at the O.K. Corral is reenacted* (opposite below left) *several times a day. At other hours Tombstone is peacefully populated by prospectors adding atmosphere, and stagecoach and covered wagon drivers offering rides* (opposite above and opposite below right).

(named after Doc Holliday's girlfriend), in the former Grand Hotel (built in 1881), and the Crystal Palace, with its original wooden back bar and hanging gas-style lamps. The gambling tables are gone, though, and the "bar girls" tend the tables with tongues firmly in cheek.

The Bird Cage Theatre, where Lillian Russell sang and Little Egypt danced, is another museum of sorts, displaying curtained compartments suspended from the ceiling where ladies of the evening offered other forms of entertainment.

A block away is the *Tombstone Epitaph*, the newspaper founded in 1880 by John Clum, who had come to Arizona as an agent at the San Carlos Reservation. A vocal Republican and one-time mayor of Tombstone, Clum would sell the *Epitaph* two years later. But while he was in town, he made his paper a voice against the lawless "cowboys," who were rustling cattle, robbing stagecoaches, and threatening relations with Mexico by crossing the border; a rival daily, the Democrat-supporting *Nugget,* tended to back the cowboys.

Of all Tombstone's characters, the most famous are the Earps. Wyatt, a former lawman, became part-owner of a saloon and rode shotgun for Wells Fargo. James owned his own saloon. Virgil was deputy marshal, sometimes aided by Morgan. Throughout 1881 the brothers tangled with the cowboy faction, especially the Clantons and the McLaurys, until on October 26th the bad blood rose to the surface. What the world knows as the "Gunfight at the O.K. Corral," however, actually took place outside it, on Fremont Street.

There Wyatt, Virgil, and Morgan Earp and Doc Holliday faced off against Ike and Billy Clanton and Frank and Tom McLaury. There were words, threats, and gunshots. Thirty seconds later it was over – though the controversy over who fired first and why has lasted more than a century. Frank, Tom, and Billy were dead; Virgil, Morgan, and Doc were wounded. The Earps were arrested and charged with murder, but a judge eventually cleared them. That wasn't the end: two months later, after Virgil had been shot and crippled,

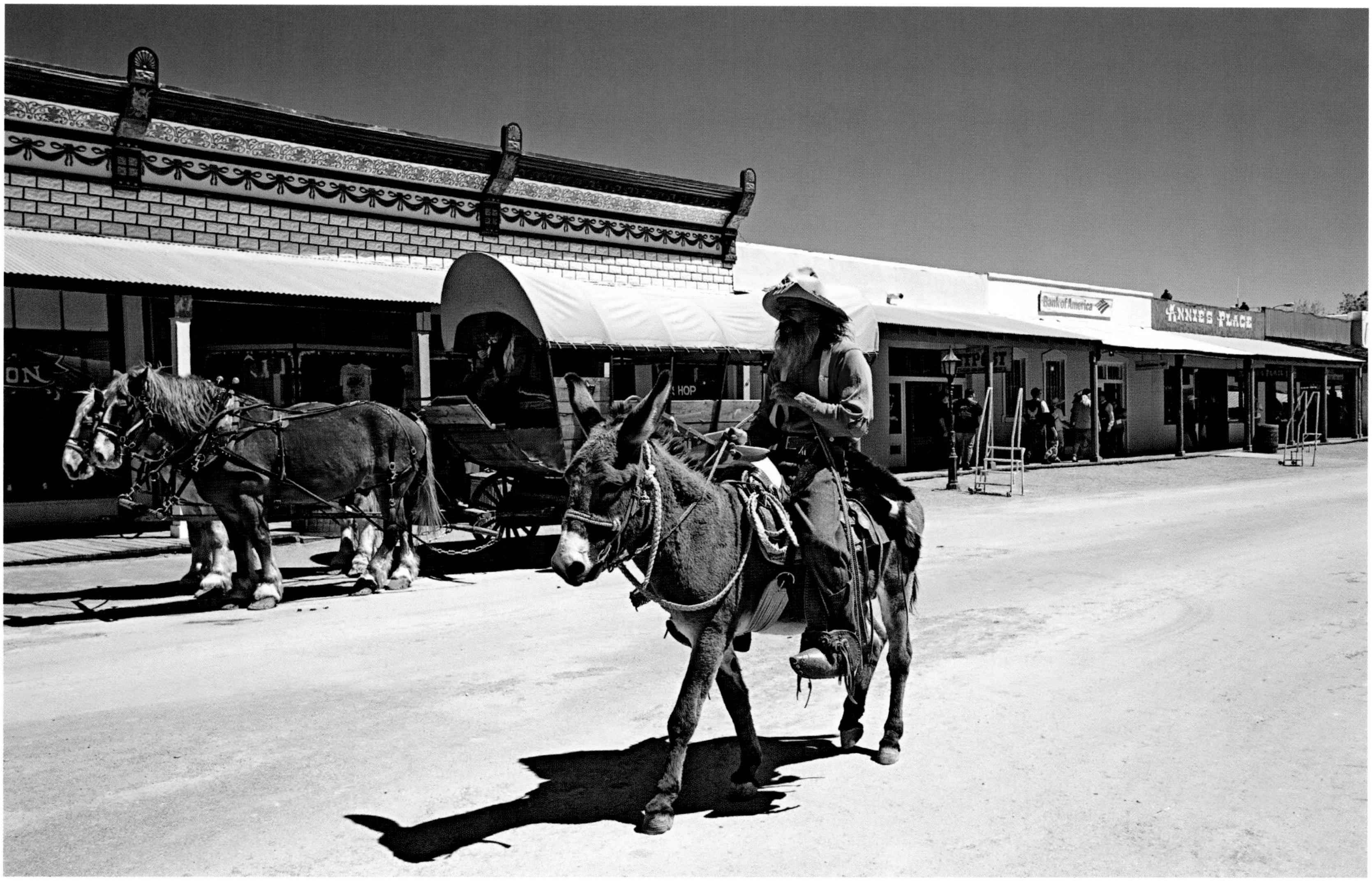
Bank of America
ANNIE'S PLACE

O.K. CORRAL
C. S. Fly Photographer
ORIENTAL
SALOON
The Tombstone Epitaph

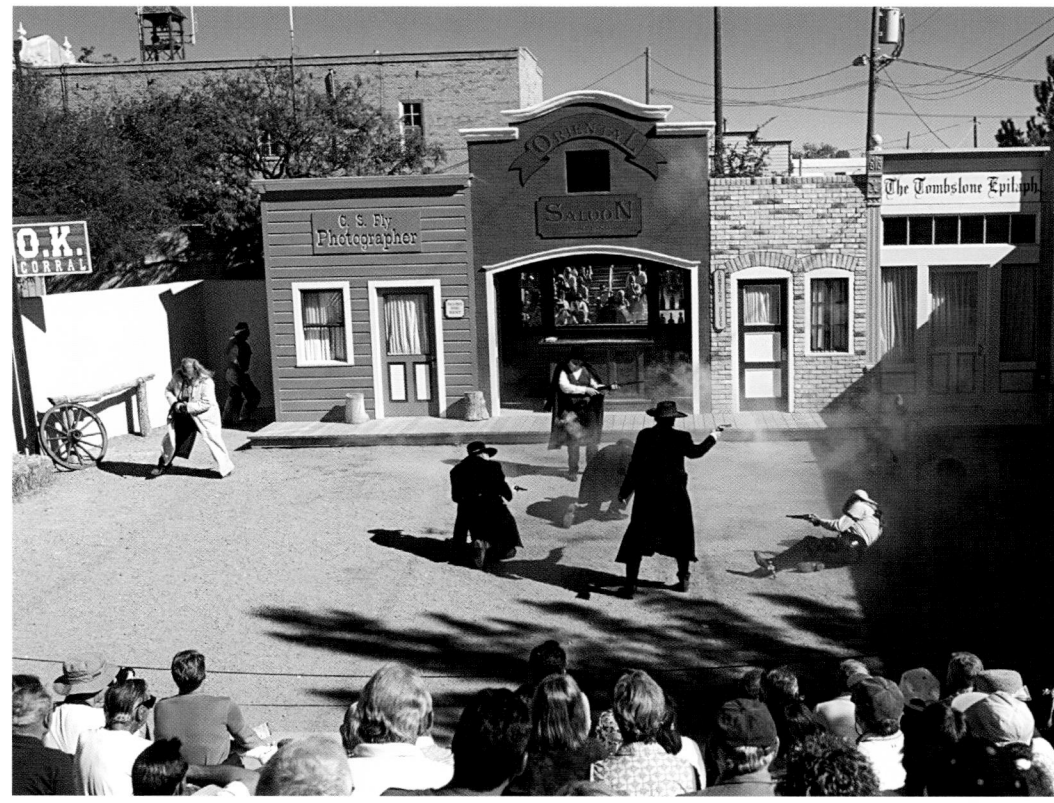

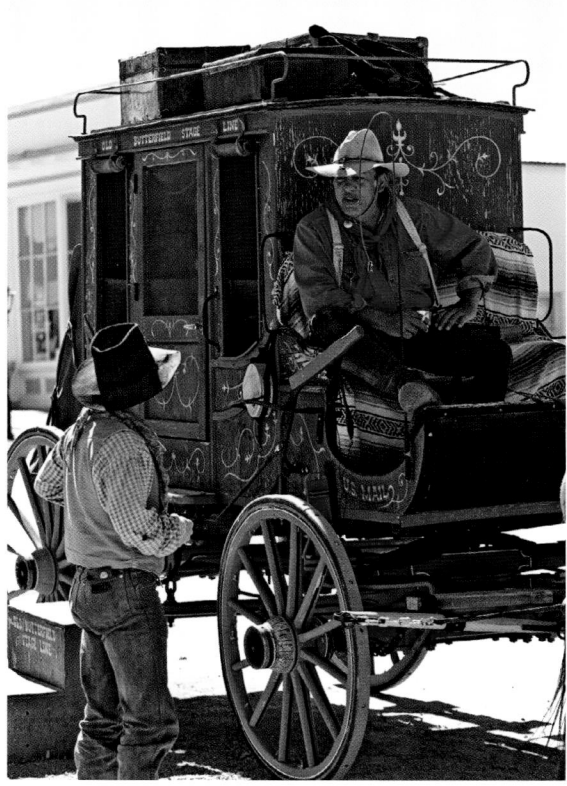

Outside after dark, electric lights delineate Allen Street's false-front façades (opposite), *including the 1881 Grand Hotel that is now Big Nose Kate's Saloon. Indoors, at the Crystal Palace* (above), *however, the decor is 19th-century gaslight, with the added attraction of "bar girls" in costume* (near left). *The raunchy touches are meant in good fun, as the sign for a local B & B demonstrates* (far left).

Wyatt took over as deputy marshal, pursuing the cowboys relentlessly, until, in March of 1882, Morgan was killed by a gunshot through a saloon window. The Earps left Tombstone shortly thereafter.

The McLaurys and Billy Clanton are still there, however, in three of the more than 250 graves that form orderly rows on Tombstone's Boot Hill.

Tumacácori & Tubac

A floral cross (opposite) *graces the centuries-old adobe-brick entry of the mission at Tumacácori National Monument* (above) *after a ceremony. No longer a church, the building still has an awe-inspiring serenity.*

A SENSE OF grace envelops the old mission church at Tumacácori, though the façade is missing chunks of limestone plaster around its arched entrance, and the square bell tower never got its intended dome. Inside, the nave is surprisingly narrow, with exposed brick on the walls and a pulpit jutting from a corner under the high, flat ceiling. Traces of the original painted decorations – a chalice and grapes, garlands of local plants – show faintly in places. No one has worshiped here for more than 150 years, yet a feeling of spirituality hangs in the air, defying the ravages of time and the weight of history.

The missionary presence in Tumacácori is even older than this church, dating back as early as 1691, when the Jesuit Eusebio Kino traveled north from Mexico to convert the Pima Indians who lived here in the shadow of the San Gabriel mountains. His padres put up a small sanctuary, planted gardens and orchards, and established a self-sustaining community on the eastern bank of the Santa Cruz river, one of many missions

that extended the reach of Spain to this part of the New World.

Kino died in 1711, and 40 years later, after decades of increasing resentment of the Spanish encroachment, the Pima rebelled. Though their revolt lasted only four months, 50 soldiers arrived in 1752 to construct a presidio at Tubac, just a few miles away. The priests moved across the river to the mission's present site, and from that day on, the fate of Tumacácori and Tubac were intertwined, both communities prospering and failing as local and international events affected them.

In the mid-18th century, Tubac – where the foundations of the original barracks and captain's house are on view in the Presidio State Historic Park – was a dusty, remote outpost harassed by the Apaches who had recently drifted into the area. The able Spanish captain Juan Bautista de Anza II arrived as commander in 1760 and stayed 16 years. From Tubac he would lead two expeditions overland to the Pacific, bringing soldiers

The Festival de Tumacácori brings in the San Carlos Apache Crown Dancers (below), fry-bread makers (bottom), and a vividly costumed Mexican folkloric group (opposite above).

and settlers to found San Francisco. In 1776 the Tubac garrison was pulled back to Tucson; without protection, the Spanish farmers who had clustered around the fort moved away, returning only in 1787, when a new company was posted to the presidio. Don Toribio de Otero was one of the Spanish settlers granted a house site and land, which would form the basis of a vast cattle empire more than a century later.

Meanwhile, Franciscans had supplanted the Jesuits at Tumacácori. Though the number of their converts was

South-of-the-border pottery shops fill Tubac's plaza (above), not far from the centuries-old Presidio park, where military reenactors (opposite below) fire a cannon as part of Anza Days festivities.

dwindling, the padres began to construct a handsome new sanctuary in 1800. It would never be completely finished, due to lack of money and the Mexican struggle for independence from Spain, but beginning in 1822 services were held there anyway. In 1848, after a harsh winter, numerous Apache raids, and a lack of supplies because of the Mexican–American War, the mission at Tumacácori was abandoned, and the residents of Tubac fled once more.

With the Gadsden Purchase of 1853, this slice of land – part of New Mexico Territory at the time – passed to the United States. A new wave of entrepreneurs entered the scene under the aegis of the Sonora Exploring and Mining Company, which set up shop in the old presidio. Houses were built on the surrounding streets, and the *Weekly Arizonian* began to publish the news. The paper's printing press is also on display in the Presidio State Historic Park, along with artifacts, clothes, and several buildings representing various eras of settlement in Tubac. The mining bonanza was short-lived, though, and by the Civil War Tubac again had declined, though it never completely disappeared.

Two silos account for the name of a restaurant (below) at the Tubac Golf Resort. Near the mission, a pool hall bears its owner's moniker: Abe's Old Tumacacori Bar (bottom).

For a century the town maintained the air of a quiet Mexican village, and with the end of World War II, its peaceful atmosphere and lovely setting attracted first artists and then retirees. The village has since spread from the original presidio to include a modest plaza and half a dozen streets lined with galleries, pottery-

and metalwork boutiques, jewelers, cafés and bookstores. It's an active, thriving community of painters and sculptors who welcome hundreds of outside artists to town during the February Festival of the Arts.

Meanwhile, at the edge of town, cows still roam the old Otero Ranch, but they're cleared from the fairways every morning. The property has become a golf resort – and was used as a filming location for the Kevin Costner movie *Tin Cup* – with an elegant restaurant in the estate's historic stables. If Tumacácori is a place frozen in time, then Tubac has moved, with utter relaxation, into the 21st century.

Cows add a bucolic – and historic – touch to a golf course (above) *that once was part of the 19th-century Otero Ranch.*

Monument Valley and Beyond
The Southwest and the Movies

The scenic outlooks in the Navajo Tribal Park, astride the Arizona–Utah border, bear colorful titles suggested by the desert: Elephant Butte, Three Sisters, North Window, and the Thumb. One of them, though, is John Ford's Point, named for the director who used Monument Valley as his shooting location for seven classic films and in the process fused the views from that spot indelibly with our images of the Southwest.

At John Ford's Point the panorama focuses on Merrick Butte, a solid rectangular block of rust-colored sandstone. Equally famous in Monument Valley are the Mittens, East and West, which thrust their ruddy hands skyward in an eternally photogenic salute. It was landscapes like these that brought Hollywood calling. The Goulding family who ran the trading post in Monument Valley and the Parry brothers in Kanab, Utah, actually lobbied directors with photos, enticing them to come out on location. With such unforgettable backdrops, it wasn't long before the movie scenery dominated our collective vision of the region, coloring what we expected to see and hoped to experience there.

Ford's first movie in Monument Valley was *Stagecoach*, in 1939, which launched both John Wayne and the "set" to stardom. Wayne returned to the area to act in the director's cavalry trilogy – *Fort Apache*, *She Wore a Yellow Ribbon* (Wayne's character's quarters still stand at the Gouldings' museum), and *Rio Grande* – as well as for *The Searchers* in 1956. Ford came back, sans Wayne, for *My Darling Clementine* and *Cheyenne Autumn,* and in the decades that followed, the buttes, towers, and extraordinary vistas were featured in films as diverse as *The Eiger Sanction, Back to the Future*, and *Forrest Gump.*

Meanwhile, Wayne's roles took him to other places throughout the Southwest. You can admire his hat in a restaurant in Ouray, Colorado (*True Grit*), take your picture with a life-size cutout in a movie museum in Moab (*The Comancheros*), and sleep in a room named for him in Kanab (*The Big Trail, In Old Oklahoma,* and *El Dorado*). You can also follow Wayne to the red-rock canyons of Sedona, Arizona, where he played a gunman destined for reform in *Angel and the Badman.*

Sedona's movie connections reach back to the silent-film era, when it was the setting for the 1923 *Call of the Canyons,* with a screenplay adapted

Nature supplied a sense of drama in the buttes and canyons around Sedona (opposite)*; moviemakers did the rest. In the 1920s, a silent film was the first to be shot here; decades later the landscape rang with Elvis Presley's voice.*

When filming in the Kanab area, Hollywood actors often stayed at the Parry Lodge (above), where room names recall the famous guests.

by Zane Grey from his own novel. Unfortunately, bad weather so disrupted the shoot that filmmakers were dissuaded from returning for almost a decade. Eventually, they came back often enough to make 92 features and TV shows in Sedona, including *Johnny Guitar*, the original *3:10 to Yuma*, *Broken Arrow*, *Blood on the Moon*, and even Elvis Presley's *Stay Away, Joe*.

The Kanab area has an equally long film heritage – from Tom Mix in *Deadwood Coach* in 1924 to Tim Burton's remake of *Planet of the Apes* in 2001. Residents frequently pitched in as extras and doubles, leading to a 1949 *Life* magazine story about the local "stars." A dozen years later, Frank Sinatra and the Rat Pack came to Kanab to work on *Sergeants 3*, and the set built for that occasion remained in Paria Canyon, outside town, for decades. It was used in Clint Eastwood's *The*

Outlaw Josie Wales before the structures succumbed to flood and finally arson. However, another set, originally constructed for *Westward the Women*, is still standing along the road into Johnson Canyon, leaning a bit but nevertheless erect. Most people will recognize the weathered wood buildings as the stomping grounds of Sheriff Matt Dillon, Kitty Russell, and Doc Adams in the long-running TV show *Gunsmoke*. Keen-eyed explorers of other areas around Kanab might also spot the rocky outcrop where Clayton Moore as the Lone Ranger reared his horse to the call of "Hi-Yo, Silver!"

Directors discovered Moab, Utah, in 1949, often coupling filming there with locations in Monument Valley, whose landmarks can be seen far in the distance. The dramatic landforms around Canyonlands National Park and at Dead Horse Point offered spectacular aerial shots and precipitous drop-offs – including the famous drive-into-oblivion finale of *Thelma and Louise.*

Countless other towns throughout the Southwest have had cameos on the silver screen. For *The Milagro Beanfield War,* Robert Redford chose Truchas, New Mexico, to portray a quirky community unchanged for

Two thumbs up – the Mittens of Monument Valley (above) have earned the movie critics' unwavering approval for their appearances in countless Westerns, beginning with the classic Stagecoach, *starring John Wayne. For two decades, the* Gunsmoke *set (opposite top), near Kanab, was a fixture on television, standing in for the Dodge City stomping grounds of Marshall Matt Dillon.*

A sign at a lookout in Monument Valley Navajo Tribal Park (above) celebrates the cinematic giant who placed his director's chair here and gave the world its quintessential vision of the American Southwest.

centuries. (Nearby Chimayó turned down the honor.) Durango, Colorado, had the steam locomotives that added authenticity to the 1956 *Around the World in 80 Days* and *Butch Cassidy and the Sundance Kid*, while the Plaza Hotel in Las Vegas, New Mexico, offered atmospheric interiors for the recent Oscar-winning *No Country for Old Men*.

In 1960 the residents of Virginia City, Nevada, found the cast of *The Misfits* – including Montgomery Clift and Clark Gable – filming on their doorstep. The scenes of mustangs, canyons, low hills, and alkaline flats were shot by John Huston in shimmering black and white, but admittedly it's the memories of Marilyn Monroe, who lodged in a room in town, that have never faded.

The Misfits' elegiac tone is only one of the recurring cinematic depictions of the Southwest, which has been portrayed as romantic, heroic, rollicking, or rough, depending on the era. One thing has rarely changed, however. Say "ride into the sunset," and we all know the image that comes to mind.

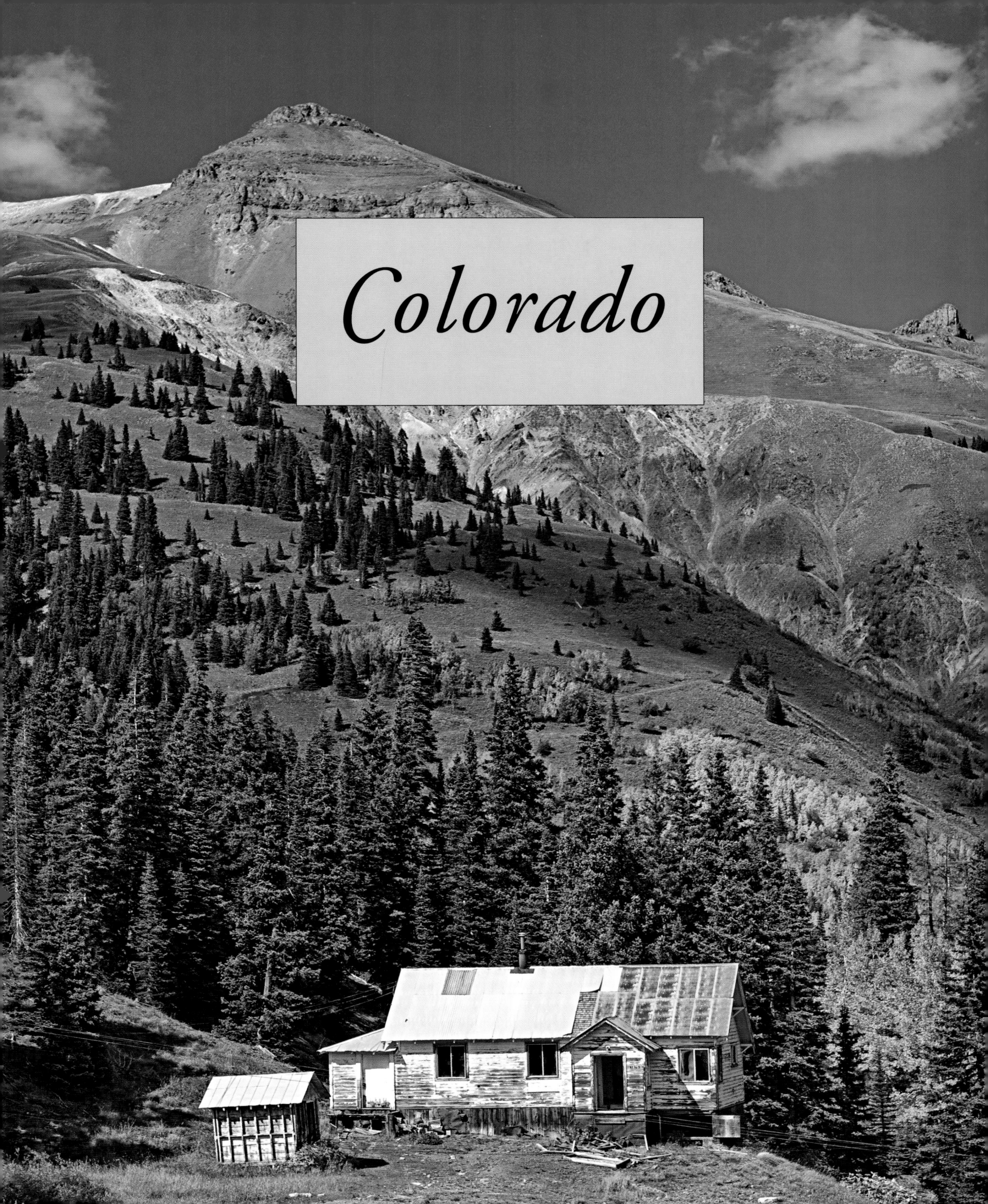

Colorado

Aspen

THE 40 VERDANT acres of the Aspen Institute edge the gracious residential streets of this chic ski town, promising – depending on the season – world-class concerts, internationally renowned conferences, or simply a Bauhaus-inspired resort setting. Established in 1950 on the premise that environment, culture, and community could be integrated and that mind, body, and spirit could flourish in this spectacular mountain setting, the Institute, led by founders Walter and Elizabeth Paepke, sparked a local renaissance that continues to this day.

The Paepkes had the vision and connections to infuse their project both with gravitas and glamour. Walter was the head of the American Container Corporation, Elizabeth a designer and art patron. When, in 1949, they organized a 200th birthday convocation in Aspen for German poet Johann Wolfgang von Goethe, even Albert Schweitzer showed up.

Walter Paepke commissioned Bauhaus architect and artist Herbert Bayer to design buildings and art for the Institute, which later shared its grounds with the Music

Festival and the Institute for Physics. The events and venues – along with new ski facilities – resuscitated a former mining community that had languished for most of the 20th century.

The town got its start in 1879, when miners from Leadville came looking for another source of silver. They found veins of incredibly rich ore, and within a year the remote, aspen-lined valley of the Roaring Fork River – once the summer hunting grounds of Ute Indians – had permanent settlers not only in Aspen but

also in camps like Ashcroft, Independence, and Ruby.

Thanks to financiers like Jerome B. Wheeler, who used his Macy's department store fortune to put his entrepreneurial stamp on the town, Aspen took precedence among the fledgling communities in the area, especially after the railroad arrived in 1887, and Wheeler completed the first local ore smelter.

In 1889 the Wheeler Opera House welcomed stars of the 19th-century "silver circuit" to a handsome peachblow sandstone building that also housed the

*O*ld mine structures endure at Red Mountain Pass, between Ouray and Silverton. (Page 55)

*A*utumn transforms Aspen's signature trees (opposite) into groves of gold. It was a silver boom, however, that made the town prosperous and led to the wealth of industrial Victorian buildings along Galena Street (above).

The epitome of luxury and up-to-the-minute amenities when it opened in 1889, the Hotel Jerome (above) again is a sparkling fixture among accommodations in Aspen. Visiting glitterati find high fashion downtown (left) along with old-style transportation (opposite) if they've shopped till they dropped.

Wheeler Bank. That same year the Hotel Jerome – also named for Wheeler – opened its doors as a first-class inn, complete with hot and cold water, steam heat, and electric lights. Though the opera house was later damaged by fire and ravaged by years of neglect, its auditorium now shines with tiny silver stars on its teal-colored walls, and noted performers bring in the crowds. As for the hotel, its lobby is once again resplendent, with overstuffed Victorian settees, a carved wood fireplace, and gilt mirrors.

Wheeler also built a Queen Anne mansion for his family, though they never lived in the house as his wife refused to move from their home in Manitou Springs. Today the Wheeler-Stallard House (denoting the family that bought it in 1925) is a museum for the Aspen Historical Society. The group's costumed docents also conduct tours of the historic district, recounting colorful tales about the fine architecture that was funded by the town's mineral wealth.

The Pitkin County Courthouse, for example, with its glorious purple tower, displays a somewhat cynical silver statue of Justice without her blindfold, and the sandstone-and-brick Elks Building, from 1891, has a landmark silver dome. In the 19th century Aspen was a rough, hard-working industrial place, though, with smelters, mills, and a railroad, as well as drinking establishments and other entertainments. In 1893, however, the repeal of the Sherman Silver Purchase Act knocked the bottom out of the silver market. Aspen's boom times were over…for a while.

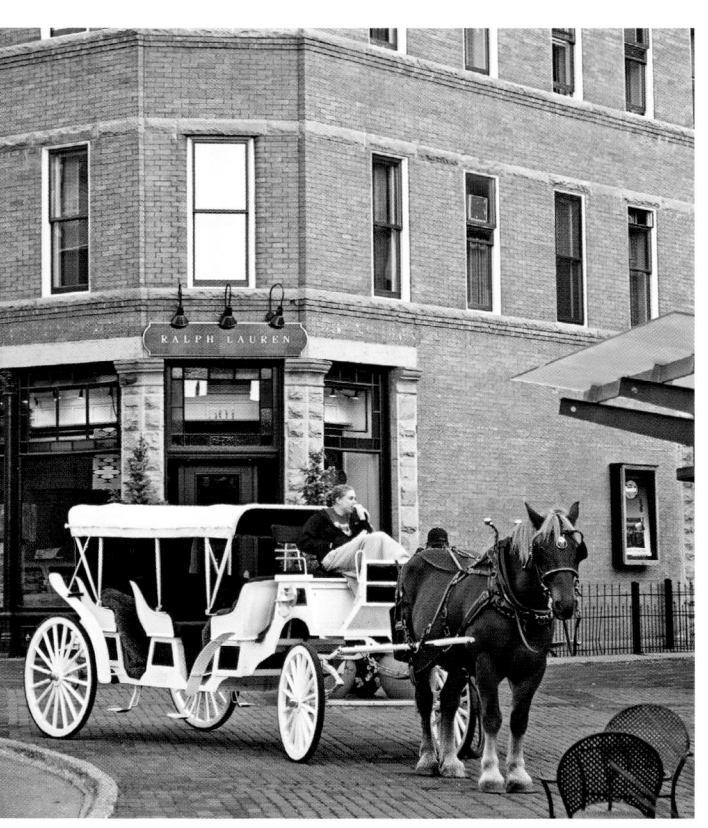

For the next several decades, valley residents survived on ranching and Aspen's position as a county seat. In the mid-1930s the area attracted international interest as a potential ski resort, but World War II put an end to that. Yet the sport began to take hold in the area, as enthusiasts built a race course up Aspen Mountain and rigged a "boat tow" to get people up the slopes. Local skiers were joined by soldiers from the 10th Mountain Division, who came to train as alpinists – and in their free time popularized "Aspen crud," a milkshake concoction laced with bourbon that was served in the Hotel Jerome's J-Bar.

After the war, skiing turned out to be the sports component Walter Paepke envisioned for the new Aspen. With his support, in 1947, noted skier Friedl Pfeifer inaugurated the first chair lift here, which offered a cold 45-minute ride to the mountaintop. Within 20 years, three other mountains opened for skiing, and Aspen acquired an aura of glitz, both on the slopes and in its après-ski scene. Gradually dilapidated properties were bought up and renovated, though a healthy contingent of iconoclasts – Hunter Thompson

Scales in hand, a silver statue of Justice warily keeps her eyes open, as she presides in front of the Pitkin County Courthouse (above), *built in 1891 amid controversy over political shenanigans.*

famously held court in neighboring Woody Creek – and a strong current of environmental concern also shaped the town's modern persona.

Today Aspen is a cherished vacation spot for lovers of ideas, music, shopping, and the great outdoors. Fly-fishermen prize its streams, well-used bike paths criss-cross the valley, and the Snowmass ski area is being revitalized along sustainable lines. In town,

An easy street for pedestrians, the historic commercial blocks of the Hyman Avenue Mall (left) offer extraordinary window-shopping. A gallery on the next street is artfully inviting (above), while the J-Bar (top) is a perennially favorite watering hole.

19th-century structures have become Prada, Burberry, and Ralph Lauren boutiques, as well as gourmet restaurants owned by celebrity chefs. The old saloon district boasts five-star hostelries, while every other storefront seems to be a real estate office touting multimillion-dollar residences – or sites to build them on.

Yet the splendor of the mountainous backcountry that awaits a few miles outside of town remains undimmed. Thousands of travelers now visit the meadows below the jagged heights of the Maroon Bells, where the view of those 14,000-foot peaks is still an exhilarating gift to mind, body, and spirit.

The alpine peaks of the Maroon Bells (right) draw outdoor enthusiasts to hike, bike, picnic, and ski the backcountry. In the late 1800s the mining settlement of Ashcroft (below and bottom) had 6 hotels and 17 saloons. Today only a few eerily empty structures survive.

Breckenridge

THE MASSIVE BARRIER of the Ten Mile Range scrapes the sky beyond Breckenridge like a scalloped wall. The peaks, still stunningly white after a long snow-filled winter, rise more than 13,000 feet, but even the town's broad valley lies at 9,600 feet in elevation. The scene immediately makes you wonder how people could live here…and why?

The first answer, of course, is gold. In 1859, prospectors came here in search of the nuggets that dotted the Blue River and other nearby streams. Within a year the camp boasted several thousand residents, but a year later the easy gold had been panned out, and people began to drift away, setting a pattern of boom and bust that was to characterize the place's history.

By then the town had a post office, established, some think, after locals flatteringly named their new home for Vice President John Breckinridge. The "i" was later changed to an "e," it's said, when the honoree revealed

his Confederate sympathies. Or perhaps spelling was more casual in those days. No matter – Breckenridge it would be.

By 1870 the population had dwindled to just 51 souls, but hydraulic technology made gold mining feasible again in the area, and gave the settlement a needed boost. The Lomax Placer Mine Site at the edge of town shows how people lived and worked in those days, with a typical bare-bones miner's cabin and the Tiger Mine assay office. A bearded interpreter demonstrates panning and shows off an early sluice box before explaining how high-pressure pipes blasted away hillsides to free the ore. It wasn't just gold that the prospectors were after; there was also silver, lead, and molybdenum (a metal used in steel alloys and cast iron). To get at these metals, though, deeper mines –

The cupola of the Summit County Courthouse (above) towers over the storefronts of Lincoln Avenue. When Masons laid the cornerstone in 1909, they mixed in gold dust. Prospectors first discovered nuggets in the Blue River (above right); dredges – like the replica that houses a restaurant (right) – pulled them out until 1942.

and pockets – were needed, prompting prospectors to pool their claims and sell to bigger companies.

Meanwhile in Breckenridge, as in most mining towns, entrepreneurs were finding it was more lucrative to "mine the miners." Main Street is lined with the commercial structures – saloons, hotels, general stores, and other businesses – they built in the late 1800s, often with tall false fronts that added a sense of stature. Today the buildings are decorated with lively Victorian-style paint combinations, but contemporary wares fill the plentiful boutiques, galleries, sports shops, and restaurants. The old Gold Pan saloon, though, still has its antique mahogany back bar – and a liquor license that dates back more than a century.

The successful merchants built their residences on quieter streets to the east. Barney Ford, an enterprising African-American and one of Breckenridge's most noted citizens, prospered with his famed Chophouse restaurant and commissioned a five-room cottage in 1882. The home is now a museum that pays tribute to Ford's remarkable career – from runaway slave, to businessman, to proponent of Colorado statehood.

A statue in front of the bay-windowed Barney Ford House (above) honors the man who was born a slave and rose to become an entrepreneur and an early advocate for civil rights. The home he commissioned from architect Elias Nashold is now a museum with memorabilia and photographs (left). Breckenridge has hundreds of historic buildings. The Prospector (opposite) was a restaurant as early as 1902, connected to a miners' boarding house upstairs.

*S**now brightens the ridge of the Ten Mile Range* (above), *behind the characteristic false fronts of Main Street* (below)*, where a peaked façade would denote a residence instead of a business.*

There were lots of memorable characters in Breckenridge's early days. The Engle brothers, who were Swiss immigrants, ran a pool parlor and saloon where the stately brick courthouse now stands. More trusted than bankers, they willingly stored miners' gold dust and nuggets in their vault, and eventually they started a bank

of their own in the handsome Exchange building. Their sister, Katie, married their cashier George Briggle, and the Briggle House, too, has become a museum, complete with pot-bellied stove, old gaslight chandeliers, an organ, and the upright piano on which Katie gave lessons. Much simpler accommodation from the period is preserved in the tiny woodshed-like cabin that was home to the Methodist minister John Lewis Dyer, who traveled on rudimentary skis as he carried the word of the Lord – as well as the U.S. Mail – to remote mining camps.

The narrow-gauge railroad came to Breckenridge in 1882, thanks to an engineering feat that took the high line over Boreas Pass. Sixteen years later, mining companies began dredging gold from the Blue River bottom. The process sustained the mining industry here for more than 40 years, but the waste turned the river into an expanse of raw gravel. World War II ended mining completely, and once again Breckenridge's population fell, until in 1960 only 300 residents remained. On the west side of town, where the smelters, mills, miners' tents, and red-light district had been, little was left standing, though Main Street's buildings and the upscale east side residences survived.

Throughout the decades the Ten Mile Range had always beckoned, but it soon promised riches of a

different kind. Two Norwegians, Sigurd Rockne and Trygve Berg, began to build ski facilities, and in December 1961 Peak 8 opened, ushering in a new era. The empty side of the valley floor eventually filled with lodgings for the thousands of winter sports enthusiasts who came to ski and, after 1984, to snowboard on newly accessible runs and terrain parks.

The ski slopes provide a gorgeous backdrop to the Blue River Plaza, a pleasant open square bordered by restaurants and shops, next to the waterway that once again flows through the heart of Breckenridge. Determined and innovative environmental planning has restored the river, and residents have added sculpture, a walking trail, and benches, inviting passers-by to – why not?– stay a while.

The Exchange (left) *was established as a bank in 1880 by former saloonkeepers, who found themselves looking after gold dust deposits left by their customers. The offices inside now trade in real estate, today's valuable commodity in this acclaimed ski resort town. Below: A horse-drawn carriage offers a slow-paced scenic tour.*

Durango & Silverton

WITH THE SOUND of a whistle and the call "all aboard!" a steam locomotive chugs out of Durango's historic depot and down a narrow-gauge track, past a gauntlet of photographers intent on recording the sight. The scene is repeated several times a day in summer as the trains of the Durango & Silverton Railroad embark on their scenic 45-mile run.

Next to the yellow clapboard station, which was built in 1881, is a cavernous museum housed in a 20-year-old reconstructed brick roundhouse that serves as shelter for the line's working locomotives and a private rail car. In fact, the museum is a functioning train yard – complete with maintenance and machine shops, a turntable, and storage.

The railroad was founded by General W. J. Palmer, a Civil War hero who built a narrow-gauge line from Denver to Colorado Springs and later envisioned a route to Silverton, at the center of the ore-rich, but road-poor, mining camps in the San Juan Mountains.

Silverton had had a brief gold rush in 1860, when Charles Baker led a group of prospectors to what was then Ute territory. The Civil War quickly ended plans

for more mining, but in 1870 the miners trickled back. Three years later, when the Native Americans, led by Chief Ouray, signed a treaty giving up the area, settlers poured in. This time the miners found silver – "by the ton!" as one man supposedly exclaimed.

By 1875 Silverton had 100 buildings, including a school and a post office, and its spectacular mountains were staked with mining claims. Life was rugged and hard enough in summer; in winter, snows and avalanches often cut off supplies for months, adding to the costly problem of shipping out ore.

The enterprising Otto Mears constructed a network of toll roads connecting Silverton and its mining districts to Ouray in the north and to Animas City in the south. But only a railroad would drop freight costs dramatically. That's where General Palmer came in.

Bypassing agricultural Animas City in favor of starting its own town a few miles away, Palmer's Denver and Rio Grande Railroad established Durango in 1880 and began laying tracks to the north. By July 1882, the line had reached Silverton, ushering in several decades of prosperity periodically interrupted by low ore prices.

A revived relic of the past, a steam locomotive carries tourists on the narrow-gauge track (above) between Durango and the depot in tiny Silverton (above left). Winter snows halt the trips but attract extreme skiers who have discovered the appeal of the surrounding mountains.

Galleries, restaurants, and boutiques fill other historic sites, while the Silverton Jail, located next to the gold-domed courthouse, has been reconstituted as a local museum. One block over is Blair Street, the town's notorious red-light district, where the wooden false-front façades denoted bars, gambling dens, dance halls, and dubious boarding houses for "soiled doves."

While Silverton mined its mountain lodes, Durango prospered as a regional rail hub, where mills and smelters were built to process the ore. It had its own fine buildings, like Henry Strater's grand brick hotel, which went up in 1887 at the corner of Main Avenue and Seventh Street. Today the beautifully renovated lobby is once again a popular meeting place, and the guest rooms are furnished with antique four-poster beds. On the corner, in the hotel's Diamond Belle Saloon, bar girls in 1890s dresses continue the Victorian theme.

Outside the hotel, the Main Avenue storefronts showcase several decades of commercial architecture, with arched windows, decorative cornices, and cast-iron façades. Third Avenue, however, was the residential neighborhood favored by Durango's upper class. It still is distinguished by elaborate Victorian mansions as well as classic cottages and bungalows.

In the 20th century the narrow-gauge line between Durango and Silverton changed ownership and declined along with the mining industry. For decades it seemed as though the railroad, too, would disappear, but in 1981 it was revived as a historical tourist attraction. Meanwhile, Durango and Silverton, forever linked by rail, have followed their own distinct paths.

Though the repeal of the Sherman Silver Purchase Act in 1893 turned outlying settlements into ghost towns, Silverton mined enough other minerals to survive.

The results are visible in the solid Victorian buildings along Greene Street, the main thoroughfare in a historic district that takes in the entire town. Silverton's Grand Imperial Hotel, for example, is a memorably ornate three-story structure that dates to 1882. Renovated over the last 15 years, the hotel includes a saloon that makes a perfect backdrop for the pianist who bangs out ragtime tunes at lunchtime.

*T**he grand lobby of Durango's Strater Hotel* (above) *was a place for locals to meet and discuss mining issues of the late 1800s. Renovated a decade ago, the room preserves the chandeliers from the town's demolished courthouse as well as a glass case with a corset supposedly left by actress Lillian Russell. Old-time atmosphere in Silverton extends from a turn-of-the-century brick façade* (right) *to the pleasures of an ice cream parlor inside.*

*C*ars and trucks add a
contemporary touch to
Silverton's historic district, where
the blue-and-white Grand Imperial
Hotel majestically anchors a corner
of Greene Street (above). Durango's
Main Avenue (right) was part of
a grid laid out by railroad officials
who founded the town in 1880.
This was – and is – the lively
business district; two blocks away
gracious residences line quieter
Third Avenue.

*T*rails *for four-wheeling excitement lead to a waterfall near Clear Lake* (opposite) *and to California Gulch* (above). *Two-wheel aficionados explore the abandoned mine buildings in the ghost town of Animas Forks* (left).

The mining industry ended once and for all in Silverton when the Sunnyside Mine closed in 1991. Remote, quiet, with a frozen-in-time feel, the town is a bit like Brigadoon, coming to life each time the train pulls into town. The few hundred residents are joined by ten times that number every summer. And in winter, the snowy slopes of Silverton's 13,000-foot mountains are beginning to attract extreme sports enthusiasts and heli-skiers, who find the rugged environment a world-class challenge.

In Durango, restaurants, breweries, coffee shops, and galleries fill the town's historic buildings, and the streets have a youthful vibe, accentuated by the students who attend Fort Lewis College. The landscape inspires exuberance, tempting you to try a mountain bike ride or a river raft trip, unforgettable experiences that raise your spirits as high as the surrounding hills.

Georgetown & Idaho Springs

THIRTY MILES WEST of Denver, pine-covered mountains loom on two sides of Clear Creek, creating a narrow canyon at the town of Idaho Springs. These days, as the weather warms, the river attracts throngs of rafters eager to test themselves on the rapids that churn with the spring runoff.

A century and a half ago, it was the river that gave birth to the town. In January 1859 George A. Jackson was on a hunting trip when he panned some gold from the stream with his drinking cup. Jackson returned with a party of would-be miners in the spring, and the Colorado gold rush was on.

Up to then, Idaho Springs had been populated only by Ute Indians, who came to use the natural hot springs. Now the new town grew steadily, from 400 residents around 1860 to 14,000 in the early 1900s. Its prosperity was based on the mines – which were aided by the arrival of the railroad in 1877 – and the good times of the 1870s and 1880s are reflected in the handsome storefronts of Miner Street, as well as the turn-of-the-century residences that grace Colorado Boulevard.

Many historic buildings have been imaginatively adapted for 20th-century uses. The old brick schoolhouse, with its open bell tower, was renovated to become City Hall; a former sweet shop now houses a dentist's office; and a mercantile warehouse has been transformed into an antique store full of gleaming cast-iron stoves. A dry-goods store, a saloon, and a billiard parlor were combined to form the Buffalo Bar and Restaurant, whose buffalo-painted wooden doors swing open to an atmospheric eatery.

In a nod to the mining that continue into the 1940s, the 1911 home and office of mining engineer James Underhill have also been preserved, complete with the vault, weights, and ore samples of his profession, and the gracious furnishings – including a spinet piano – that characterized refined domestic life.

A dozen miles west of Idaho Springs, Georgetown was another product of the Colorado gold rush, but the settlement nearly died out, until the discovery of silver in 1864 brought about a revival. William Hamill, for one, prospered as the owner of mines, a smelter, and a quarry, and served as railroad commissioner and state senator. His gorgeous Gothic Revival residence, built in 1867 and enlarged in 1879, has ornate wallpaper and fancy cornices in the parlor, a stone fireplace in the dining room, a library with leather sofas, and a glass-walled conservatory filled with greenery. The meticulously renovated house is now the centerpiece of

*L*ocally made brick went into the fine Victorian shop fronts of Miner Street (opposite), the heart of Idaho Springs' historic district. There four adjoining buildings make up the Buffalo Restaurant (left) where a mural carries on the bison theme. The water wheel now located on Clear Creek (above left) once powered a stamp mill for gold, the source of the town's 19th-century prosperity.

Georgetown's charming Sixth Street (above) *extends to the Star Hook and Ladder Company, with its open bell tower. Across the way is the Hotel De Paris Museum* (opposite). *The Hamill House parlor* (left) *also showcases the swank 19th-century lifestyle.*

Historic Georgetown, Inc, which also owns a mine manager's Queen Anne villa, a merchant's residence, a simple miner's cottage, and a log cabin, all representative of the town's varied 19th-century lifestyles.

By 1875, well-off visitors could stay at the sumptuous Hotel De Paris, the creation of Louis DuPuy, a French chef and entrepreneur. Born Adolph Gerard, he changed his name on the way to the Colorado mines, then turned a bakery into a noted two-story inn and restaurant. You can tour his elegant dining room set with fine china, see his zinc baker's table, and marvel at the rooms he cleverly outfitted for visiting salesmen to show off their wares.

In 1893, the price of silver plummeted, closing most of Georgetown's mines. Slowly the town declined, though, thanks to its four hose companies, the trove of turn-of-the-century architecture never succumbed to

*M*ine owner and civic leader William Hamill bought the mansion on Argentine Street (above) and later added touches – like the fountain and conservatory – he'd admired at a world's fair. The 1870s wood-frame homes of Taos Street (left) also have individualized details.

fire. Among hundreds of eye-catching structures in the historic district are the Kniesel-Anderson Grocery, where four generations of one family have served customers from behind the same glass counters; the Maxwell House with a pink-and-chocolate color scheme on its Victorian gingerbread; and the Alpine Hose No. 2 Firehouse, whose distinctive tall tower was used for drying the hoses.

Another important piece of local history is the Georgetown Loop Railroad, once part of the Colorado Central that was supposed to connect to silver-rich Leadville. The narrow-gauge line was never completed, but in 1884 it did reach Silver Plume, two miles from Georgetown and 650 feet up, on a track that looped over itself on a thrilling 300-foot-long "high bridge" 100 feet above a daunting gorge.

*S*hort but sweet, the Georgetown Loop Railroad (above) *runs to Silver Plume and back on a scenic stretch of narrow-gauge track. Mining was paramount here when consulting engineers built the Teal Building* (right) *as offices in 1875.*

As the loads of ore decreased, the railroad increasingly carried tourists, though they, too, disappeared as automobiles became more prevalent. In 1939, the track was finally dismantled. Yet that wasn't the end of the railroad. Decades later, lobbying by rail buffs led the Colorado Historical Society to acquire the route, and Navy Seabees began reconstruction of the track in 1973. By 1985 even the high bridge had been rebuilt.

Today a conductor in a black vest and hat once again punches your ticket as you board vintage cars behind a steam locomotive. The four-mile trip between the historic Silver Plume depot and Georgetown's Devil's Gate Station takes you past the entrance to the Lebanon Silver Mine, across the looping bridge above the Clear Creek gorge, on a journey into the past.

Ouray

The popular path to Box Canyon Falls leads upwards, between soaring walls of rock, to a view of Canyon Creek rushing into a dark pool below. A slightly steeper trail takes you even higher, to a vertigo-inducing bridge that spans the gorge. Across the valley, on the flank of one of the alpine peaks that give this town the nickname "Switzerland of America," you can make out Cascade Falls and the tin-roofed remains of the Chief Ouray Mine.

Box Canyon was discovered in 1875 by two of the prospectors who had forged a path over the daunting San Juan Mountains in search of silver. For generations this valley had been summer grounds for the nomadic Ute Indians, who found game plentiful and used the area's many hot springs as medicinal baths for their horses. In the face of white encroachment, the Utes, led by the remarkable Chief Ouray, negotiated treaties to hold on to at least a portion of their traditional territory, though the agreements were repeatedly broken by settlers.

After 1873, when the Utes finally ceded possession of the San Juan Mountains, miners came from communities like Silverton, looking for new diggings. Within a few years prospectors were spending the winters in a rough camp that boasted a post office and the name Ouray. By 1877 the 400 residents could claim a school, two hotels, a sawmill, and several stores – as well as seven saloons and innumerable gambling dens and bordellos.

Returned to Victorian splendor, the lobby of the Beaumont Hotel (opposite) *includes its original banjo clock at the top of the staircase and an antique box piano; the exterior features a huge slate tower* (above). *A gilt cupola tops the former city hall* (left), *designed to resemble Philadelphia's Independence Hall.*

Adding Western atmosphere on Ouray's Main Street, a colorful livery barn (opposite), once home to the O.K. Stables, proclaims its age above the hayloft. During the town's boom times, farms and ranches sprang up to provision the miners. Within a few blocks, the orderly streetscape evolves into a rural scene (above) backed by spectacular mountains.

In the 1870s and 1880s, some say 10,000 mines existed in a 10-mile radius, though certainly not all of them were successful. The Bachelor-Smuggler Mine, however, steadily made money following its founding in 1884, producing gold and silver as well as tin and zinc.

The mine was shut down in 1988, but you can still ride a noisy, bumpy tram car 1,850 feet into the mountain, in pitch darkness, to get a feel of the hard-rock mining that took place here. In the beginning, the miners, mostly Welsh and Cornish, worked alone by candlelight, but over time improvements were introduced, including two-man teams, electric light, and hydraulic pneumatic drills that lessened the debilitating dust in the tunnels.

Getting the ore out was only the first step; it then had to be transported to a mill or smelter over roads that were steep, narrow, dangerous, or nonexistent. Russian-born entrepreneur Otto Mears engineered a lucrative system of toll roads – charging 25 cents for a carriage and four horses on what became the Million Dollar highway over Red Mountain Pass – which covered 200 miles by 1887. That same year the railroad connected Ouray to towns farther north, making the mines more profitable.

The resulting boom put money in the pockets of Ouray's residents, who built fine buildings all over town. Main Street's magnificent Beaumont Hotel was constructed in 1886–87 with a three-story atrium and a slate roof on its square corner tower. Following an award-winning renovation, the hotel once again welcomes guests to rooms appointed with four-poster beds, authentic patterned wallpaper, and Tiffany-style lamps.

Down the street is the cast-iron, cream-and-blue façade of Wright's Opera House, built in 1888, while a few blocks away, the Western Hotel, which opened four years later, maintains a Victorian frontier decor in its accommodations. Its congenial saloon also preserves the "face on the barroom floor" painted by an itinerant artist more than a century ago.

The sandstone-brick Miners Hospital from 1886 is now the historical museum, with three jam-packed floors of exhibits that range from a local soda fountain and the contents of a dry-goods emporium to a ranch household and a dentist's office. An upscale parlor from the late 19th century includes a replica of the Hope Diamond once owned by Evalyn Walsh McLean, who

inherited her wealth from her father, Tom Walsh, proprietor of the fabulous Camp Bird Mine and a noted town benefactor.

Like all of Colorado's mining towns, Ouray was affected by the fall in the price of silver after 1893, but the presence of gold and other metals helped it weather the crisis well into the 20th century. Though the population fell, the stunning natural setting drew visitors. Even in the early 1900s tourists were making the hike to Box Canyon Falls, and within a couple of decades, they were bathing at pools in the local hot springs and driving automobiles past the jaw-dropping panoramas on the Million Dollar Road.

Today Ouray's 850 residents are passionate about their little town, which boasts many 19th-century homes, a variety of art galleries, several hot springs pools, and a number of lively bistros. The winding gravel roads that used to service remote mining camps in Yankee Boy Basin or over Black Bear Pass are now jeep trails for an adventurous new generation.

Even the challenging winters have become an attraction in an era of extreme sports. Every December the canyon walls at the edge of town are sprayed with water and transformed into Ouray Ice Park, and in January well-bundled-up visitors and residents alike turn out for the annual Ouray Ice Festival to watch world-class climbers compete on the sheer icy rock.

A priceless view is the reward for driving the Million Dollar Road to Red Mountain Pass (right), where a few mine structures testify to the work that went on at 11,000 feet. Miners looking for silver also discovered Box Canyon Falls (below) in 1875.

Steamboat Springs

ON A COOL spring afternoon, a score of bathers are soaking in the rock-lined pools of Strawberry Park Hot Springs. Here, beneath spruce-covered hills, it looks as though nature herself has arranged outdoor Jacuzzis of varying sizes and at different levels, beckoning young romantic couples to the smallest, highest – and hottest – pond, while grandparents keep an eye on a couple of ten-year-olds in a cooler, larger corner. Other visitors ease in and out of the different pools, whose temperatures are controlled by sluice gates that divert the flow of the chilly stream alongside.

Strawberry Park is just one of the mineral springs of Steamboat, which have featured prominently in the history and lore of the town. The medicinal properties of the waters in this valley were one of the reasons Ute Indians traditionally came here in summer to hunt and perform ceremonies in the shadow of a majestic 10,500-foot peak. The chugging sound made by Steamboat Spring itself was responsible for the name bestowed on the place by French trappers in the 1800s.

Town founder Colonel James Crawford, who began homesteading here with his family in a log cabin in

A popular hike leads to Fish Creek Falls (left), which cascades 140 feet down a spruce-covered mountainside. At Strawberry Park Hot Springs (below), the geothermally heated mineral waters bubble up in bliss-inducing rock-lined pools.

*W*arm weather calls for breakfast alfresco on Lincoln Avenue (above), but even over the July 4th holiday, skis combined with roller blades make an appearance in Steamboat Springs, as Olympic-level athletes race through town (left).

1875, found the 102-degree waters of Heart Spring a congenial place to take a dip. A decade later he had a log bathhouse built over the geothermal pool, a forerunner of Steamboat's Old Town Hot Springs and Fitness Center.

Other settlers soon followed the Crawfords, who went on to build two more substantial dwellings that still stand on the street that bears their name. Some of the new homesteaders sought their fortunes in the gold and silver mines around Hahns Peak, 30 miles to the north. But even the miners often had to ranch or farm to survive. Before long most families were growing hay and grain for the cattle that came to be the mainstay of the economy and were frequently driven down Lincoln Avenue, Steamboat's main street, on the way to market, a tradition that is now revived every summer during the annual Cowboys' Roundup Days.

Steamboat's ranching heritage takes center stage every Fourth of July when cowboys drive cattle through downtown (top) and take part in rodeo competitions (top right). Ten-gallon hats are on sale all year at F. M. Light & Sons (above) the longtime local Western outfitter.

Half a dozen ranches around Steamboat date back a century or more. The Tread of Pioneers Museum celebrates those ranches and the town's early days with photographs, artifacts, and colorful tales. It also incorporates a 1908 Queen Anne-style home furnished with turn-of-the-century settees, beds, dinnerware, and toys. The museum even includes the easel and paints used by James Crawford's daughter Lulie, to create the wildflower paintings that hang on the walls. Another room of the museum is devoted to skiing, the sport is responsible for Steamboat's contemporary renown.

In the early 1900s, many locals used skis – which they called snowshoes – to get around in the heavy snows that covered the Yampa River Valley. Skiing was a necessity, not recreation, until 1913, when Carl Howelsen, a Norwegian circus athlete known as the Flying Norseman, arrived in Steamboat, set up a ski jump, and hurled himself down the slope and off the edge. It must have looked like fun. A year later there was a ski jump at the hill in the center of town, and Steamboat Springs not only had a Winter Carnival – which later featured a high school marching band on skis and a "lighted man" who skied down the hill wearing an illuminated suit – but also a Winter Sports Club. The club is still going strong. Its redwood lodge-like home is a landmark next to Howelsen Hill; more importantly, it has regularly turned out Olympic medalists since 1932.

Steamboat's downtown has its share of other historic buildings and institutions. The red-brick train depot that first welcomed passengers in 1909, a year after the railroad came to town, is now an arts center, while F. M. Light & Sons, the family-owned emporium founded in

1905, continues to stock a large inventory of cowboy hats, boots, and other Western wear.

Harwig's Saddlery, in a false-front building from the 1890s, has been transformed into a restaurant, as has the Albany Hotel, built in 1904, which saw duty early in the 20th century as the town's first hospital. Up and down Lincoln Avenue the low-rise structures now house bookstores, cafés, art galleries, and stylish boutiques.

In 1958 a local rancher broke ground for a ski area on Storm Mountain – later renamed Mount Werner, for a hometown ski champion – which has expanded over the last 50 years with trails over the so-called "champagne powder," as well as lifts, a terrain park, and lodgings that accommodate thousands of visitors every winter.

In the summer, other sides of Steamboat's personality take center stage. The rodeo established in 1909 brings bronco riders and calf ropers to compete on weekends. Hikers walk the easy path to Fish Creek Falls or challenge themselves, like the region's many mountain bikers, on longer, steeper Forest Service trails. The Yampa River invites kayakers and tubing aficionados to float through its rapids, providing entertainment for the patrons of several riverside restaurants in the process.

And in an activity that unites summer and winter, past and present, aspiring national ski jumpers practice their runs on Howelsen Hill, taking off down a slick plastic-covered slope and soaring through the air in aerodynamic Vs before sliding, with grace and flair, back to earth.

*S*ki jump training doesn't stop
when snow melts on Howelsen
Hill (right), where onlookers turn
out to watch athletes perfect their
form on a specially prepared slope.
Above and top: *Freestyle tubing on
the Yampa River also provides
entertainment for those on shore.*

Telluride

As THE SLEEK, space-age gondola whisks you up to Telluride's ski area, you get a spectacular bird's-eye view of the former mining town. At dusk, with streetlights glittering through the narrow box canyon and snow still covering the slopes, the scene resembles a toy town at Christmas.

Braving the mountains here has never been child's play, however. At the east end of the valley, where Bridal Veil Falls cascades over sheer rock, the craggy San Juans seem to form an impenetrable wall. In reality, arduous old mule roads thread through the Imogene and Black

Bear passes, offering challenging jeep rides for those who crave heart-stopping adventure.

Before the miners moved in, Ute Indians would camp in the valley only in the warm months, then retreat to less harsh territory in the winter. In 1872, however, a few prospectors from Silverton found enough silver here to make them want to stay. They were joined by hundreds of others after 1873, when the Utes finally signed away their claim to the area.

By 1878 the newcomers had laid out a settlement that eventually was christened Telluride, after the

mineral tellurium. (Another story – more colorful but, alas, apocryphal – claims the name was based on the miners' good luck sendoff: "To-hell-u-ride!") As toll roads and a railroad connected the town with distant mills, smelters, and markets, workers from around the world streamed in. Finns, Swedes, and Swede-Finns; Tyroleans from Italy and Austria; and Welsh and Cornish miners established enclaves of boarding houses and social organizations. In the early days, they mined mostly silver, though the repeal of the Sherman Silver Purchase Act in 1893 devastated the market for that metal. For a few years, the residents drifted away, until the mine companies turned to more lucrative gold, zinc, lead, and copper.

Life in the mining camps called for resilience and toughness of spirit. The men rode to work in ore buckets strung on cables across the valleys, while their wives set up housekeeping in drafty shacks. Harriet Fish Backus, whose husband toiled in the Tomboy Mine,

recounted her story in *Tomboy Bride.* The cabin she lived in is recreated in the Telluride Historical Museum, along with engaging exhibits that chronicle the vicissitudes of the town.

From the mid-1890s to the 1920s, despite intermittent labor problems, Telluride thrived. In 1891, a science-minded entrepreneur named Lucius Nunn, in partnership with George Westinghouse and Nicola Tesla, used alternating current from a hydroelectric plant to electrify the Gold King Mine, with astonishingly profitable results. Within three years Nunn had brought lights to the town as well.

The good times led to a spurt of construction. The Italianate brick courthouse went up in 1887, the elegant New Sheridan Hotel opened to guests in 1897, and the Sheridan Opera House welcomed theatergoers in 1913. The San Miguel Valley Bank was rich enough to kick off the career of one Robert Leroy Parker – alias Butch Cassidy – who successfully made off with

*C*olorado Avenue, built wide enough to turn horse-drawn carriages around, runs straight through the center of Telluride (above), where cyclists point up the town's environmental consciousness. The road ends in a box canyon with a view up a jagged mountainside splashed by the delicate stream of Bridal Veil Falls (right).

A tower for drying fire hoses tops the town hall (above), which started out in 1883 as the county's first school, with 53 students and one teacher. At the end of the block, the solid brick Miner's Union originally housed the hospital.

$24,000 on June 24, 1889, with several accomplices (though not yet including the Sundance Kid).

In those days, Colorado Avenue was the dividing line, literally, between the sunny and shady sides of town. To the north were wealthy neighborhoods distinguished by elegant, ornate Victorian dwellings and upper-class residents. Across the way were the working-class districts, as well as the saloons and bordellos that brought solace to a lonely male population. On the notorious stretch of Pacific Street known as

Popcorn Alley, three simple cribs once used by ladies of the night have been preserved and renovated. Nearby stands the former Silver Bell dancehall, as well as the Senate "female boarding house" run by 300-pound Big Billy, Telluride's most famous (and undoubtedly heaviest) madam.

In the late 1920s the mines began closing, and the Depression put an end to most of the others, though World War II briefly revived the mining industry in Telluride. The last mine shut down finally in 1978, but

*L*ocals begin gathering for breakfast or lunch at Baked in Telluride (top); by cocktail time the favored venue has shifted to the restored interior of the New Sheridan Bar (above).

Telluride was almost a ghost town by the late 1960s, when the first hippies arrived, looking for a remote, forgotten place to drop out. Despite the tiny population, the town was declared a National Historic Landmark District, a move that preserved its precious turn-of-the-century architecture from destruction.

Meanwhile, some locals had begun skiing in the backcountry, and their enthusiasm – and the spectacular natural setting – fostered Telluride's rebirth. In 1978 the first ski area opened on Gold Hill. Roughly a decade later, the ski resort at Mountain Village expanded the possibilities with new runs as well as homes and vacation lodgings. A film festival, a bluegrass festival, and several other celebrations soon filled the calendar in the off-season. Suddenly the community of tough mountain residents and countercultural iconoclasts was chic.

The old Victorian residences have now been superbly renovated into million-dollar dwellings, and the historic commercial buildings have been reborn as gourmet restaurants, interesting galleries, and luxurious

*F*rom elaborate Victorian residences (opposite) *to simple cottages for shady ladies* (left)*, Telluride's trove of architectural riches pervades a historic center hemmed in by mountains* (above)*.*

shops. The train depot is a fine-arts center, and every other storefront, it seems, displays real-estate listings that suggest – as local cynics have said – that the millionaire homeowners are being pushed out by the billionaires.

Still, on a summer afternoon during the Telluride Jazz Celebration, the mood in the city park is relaxed, and there's a feeling that anything goes. The dress code extends from threadbare flannel to Hawaiian shirts and designer jeans. Headgear ranges from snowboard caps to straw Panamas and balloon creations. On every side, jazz fans laze on blankets and lawn chairs or simply stand and sway to the sounds of the Neville Brothers, whose cool sounds have nothing to do with snow.

Trinidad

The Spanish Peaks rise above Trinidad (top), where the Coal Miners Memorial (opposite) pays tribute to the workers and the industry that sustained the town. Above: Namesake pavers.

YOU ALWAYS KNOW where you are in Trinidad. Since 1908, the streets of downtown have been paved with bricks stamped with the name of the town. To see what the Trinidad of that era looked like, well, you only have to glance up and down the streets that are part of an increasingly renovated historic district.

The preservation movement has been growing here since the 1950s, a decade after Arthur Roy Mitchell, a noted Western artist and Trinidad native, returned to his hometown. He moved into the 1870 Baca House – which was slated to become a parking lot – and set up a "pioneers' museum," dedicated to the Santa Fe Trail, in the servants' quarters in back.

Trinidad owed its existence to the trail. Two 19th-century wagon routes converged where Main and Commercial Streets meet. For several decades the cross-roads was mainly a spot for traders to rest before tackling treacherous Raton Pass a few miles south.

The first permanent settler is thought to have been Felipe Baca, who homesteaded here around 1861, then returned to New Mexico and eventually convinced another dozen families to relocate with him to Trinidad. Initially Baca and his wife, Dolores, lived in an old-style hacienda, but in 1873 he traded 22,000 pounds of wool – worth $7,000 – for the two-story adobe territorial residence that bears his name. Now part of the Trinidad History Museum, Baca's house is once again furnished with period pieces.

Beyond the rear garden of the Baca House is the Santa Fe Trail Museum that grew out of Mitchell's early

preservation efforts. Sophisticated exhibits focus on the people who came to Trinidad and the lives they led. By 1878 the old trail town was giving way to a rail town. Headquartered here were three immense open-range cattle ranches, which relied on the railroad to ship their livestock to market. One of the outfits, the Bloom Land & Cattle Company, was owned by a local banker, who built the 1882 mansion that today is also part of the historical museum complex.

In the 1870s, a coal industry sprang up in the hills around Trinidad, drawing immigrants from around the globe to opportunities in the mines. A coal tipple ran right through town, carrying ore to storage bins on the other side of the Purgatoire River.

The 1880s brought an affluence to Trinidad that left its mark in the fine architecture that now houses shops, restaurants, and museums. The luxurious three-story Columbian hotel anchored the main intersection. Across the street was the McCormick Building, with wide bay windows and gleaming black-and-gold detailing. Down the block stands the brick Chronicle-News Building, home to the daily paper that has been published since 1887.

The growing town enjoyed its cultural pursuits. The Jaffa brothers built an impressive opera house in 1883 that was supplanted in 1908 by the gargantuan West Theatre, later renamed the Fox Theatre, and which still shows movies. Trinidad also enjoyed its drink and other vices. West Main Street was known for saloons and other gentleman's entertainments. To keep law and order Bat Masterson was hired as marshal in 1882; he lasted a year before he was voted out of office.

Some of the buildings in downtown Trinidad displayed especially fanciful architectural touches. Old Firehouse No. 1, built in 1889 and now the Children's Museum, is a narrow brick structure topped by a metal cupola. And Temple Aaron, the synagogue for Trinidad's substantial Jewish population, is a solid square edifice with an onion dome reminiscent of Russian churches.

*B*uilt for a banker and cattle baron, the Bloom Mansion (below) – framed by the porch of the Chappell House – is part of the Trinidad History Museum, along with the two-story adobe Baca House (bottom), *next to the institution's columned bookstore.*

Away from the bustle of the town center, well-to-do residences dotted quiet neighborhood streets. The Chappell House, a grand Victorian with turned-wood decoration, was built for the city's water engineer. The Tarabino brothers used their department-store profits to put up a double-fronted Italianate mansion that's now a bed-and-breakfast.

Trinidad's golden age came to an abrupt end in 1913, when labor troubles engulfed the coalfields. That September the miners struck for better working conditions. Since most employees lived in company housing, they were forced to move to tent colonies that were the

site of frequent skirmishes. In April 1914, the strife culminated in an attack on the strikers by the Colorado National Guard that left some 20 people dead. Though the strike ended without resolution, the "Ludlow Massacre" commanded the attention of Congress and eventually led to changes in labor law.

After the 1920s the mines began to close. Celebrities like Will Rogers and Kate Smith periodically toured through town, but for decades Trinidad languished.

It always had loyal boosters, however, and one result of their work is the A. R. Mitchell Museum, which occupies the thoughtfully renovated Main Street space

where Jamieson's Department Store opened in 1906. Under a fine pressed-tin ceiling, a graceful balcony runs around three sides, marking off a space for visiting exhibits, while the first floor is devoted to Mitchell's art – from paintings to pulp Western magazine covers – along with a replica of his studio. Downstairs are photographs by Oliver Aultman, who began documenting the town's people, sites, and events in 1899, a project later carried on by his son. Many of the places in the photographs are still recognizable on the surrounding streets, reflecting Trinidad's lively fusion of past and present and its blend of heritage and vitality.

*T*wo branches of the Santa Fe Trail converged here, at the corner of Commercial and Main Streets (above). *Within a few decades wagons had been displaced by the stately sandstone First National Bank Building and the handsomely ornamented McCormick Building.*

Ghost Towns
RELICS OF BOOM AND BUST

Chipmunks and picas scamper in the meadow at Ashcroft, Colorado, undisturbed by two visitors who watch them from a wooden boardwalk. Here at 9,500 feet in early June, the aspens are just beginning to come into leaf on the mountains, and Castle Creek, at the edge of the grass, is rushing with late spring runoff.

Half a dozen teetering log buildings are spaced along the boardwalk. There's part of a cabin, a post office, a hotel with a tall false front, and the Blue Mirror Saloon, where photos are pinned to the walls and a few artifacts are on display. There's little to suggest that this deserted community was once home to more than 3,000 souls.

It was silver that brought them. The discovery of ore in the area in 1879 gave rise, within a year, to a town that eventually boasted 6 hotels, 17 saloons, and a jail. But when the railway bypassed Ashcroft for Aspen, 10 miles away, the town's fate was sealed. By 1890 most residents had moved, and a decade later Ashcroft was a ghost town, repeating a storyline familiar throughout the Southwest.

Most often a town faded away when the riches that had given birth to the place – gold, silver, copper – petered out. Sometimes the road or railway that nourished it was moved or shut down. Occasionally a disaster, manmade or natural, decimated the population and left the remaining residents with little desire to carry on. Slowly the wooden buildings weathered, collapsed, and disappeared. Old machinery rusted and corroded until it resembled fanciful sculptures more than industrial hardware. What was left – if anything – is a bracing reminder of just how fleeting human accomplishments can be.

St. Elmo is another Colorado mining town whose atmospheric cabins and church have become a tourist draw, as is Fairplay, where several dozen buildings – from a schoolhouse to a drugstore – have been gathered from around the state, filled with 19th-century objects, and opened as the South Park City Museum.

Among Nevada's ghost towns are Gold Hill, Gold Point, and Goldfield, whose names reflect the metal that was found there. At the edge of Virginia City, Gold Hill (where silver was also mined) is now mostly populated by the guests of the town's historic hotel. Gold Point, not far from

Log walls and not much else are all that's left of a cabin in Independence (opposite), *outside Aspen in Colorado. Winters at 10,900 feet drove the gold miners away in 1899, 20 years after they first settled here. Arizona's Vulture City sprang up around a mine in the 1860s and hung on into the 1890s. Several buildings – from an assay office to a bunkhouse – have retained a few sticks of furniture and other artifacts* (below).

Death Valley National Park, has miners' cabins to stay in and often serves as a backdrop for staged gunfights. Goldfield, meanwhile, retains a few residents who claim they have plans for the shuttered buildings – including a once-lavish hotel – that fill the town. Another preserved Nevada ghost town is Berlin, whose town site, stamp mill, and mine are part of the Berlin-Ichthyosaur State Park, outside Austin. And at Rhyolite, an old train station and caboose vie for attention with a 1906 "bottle house" and an open-air sculpture park.

Fruita, Utah, got its name from the orchards planted by Mormon settlers in 1878. Their orderly rows of fruit trees with now-gnarled limbs still line the road into Capitol Reef National Park, while a one-room schoolhouse is pretty much all that's left of the tiny community.

Arizona has made much of its picturesque mining towns. Chloride's mountainside mines were sources of gold, copper, and silver, but in the 1960s an artist named Roy Purcell focused instead on its huge rock boulders, which he used as canvases for his murals. Oatman was a gold-prospector's town just after the turn of the century, gaining fame in 1939 when Clark Gable and Carole Lombard spent their wedding night in the ramshackle hotel that's one of the attractions on its atmospheric main drag. (The others are the burros that pose for snapshots with carrot-

The South Park City Museum in Fairplay (opposite above) *duplicates the look of a Colorado mining town with authentic buildings, including a schoolhouse* (above). *Nearby St Elmo* (top) *maintains its streetscape but lets the* structures lean. Gold Point, Nevada, turned mining-camp cabins (left) *into accommodations, while at the Mammoth Saloon in Goldfield, Arizona* (opposite below), *it was the bartender who got the boot – dozens of them.*

Years of neglect have pushed the cabins in Animas Forks (right), *near Silverton, Colorado, to teeter toward ruin. In the cemetery at Dawson, New Mexico, however – all that remains of a once-vital community – the crosses stand straight* (below).

wielding tourists.) Near Wickenburg, Vulture City offers a walking trail around the structures that surrounded the Vulture Mine. Another ghost town called Goldfield – this one 30 miles from Phoenix – has turned its false-front façades into souvenir shops and sites for Wild West shows.

Sometimes towns actually refuse to give up the ghost. Though Jerome's population plummeted to a mere 50 people after its last mine closed in 1950, diehard residents made fun of their community's ghost-town status and eventually prompted the place's revival, first as a hippie enclave, then as an artists' colony. Similarly, the ghost towns of New Mexico's Turquoise Trail, especially Cerrillos and Madrid, have traded dependence on mining for an emphasis on New Age culture. Pottery, fiber arts, metal sculpture, and jewelry are on display in the colorful cottages that once were miners' homes, while saloons and mercantiles have been reopened as cafés and an occasional holistic healing center.

However, nothing remains of the New Mexico coal town of Dawson except its lonely cemetery. Once 7,000 people, predominantly European emigrants, lived here in the shadow of a sandstone bluff dotted by piñon and juniper. In the 1920s there were enough families to warrant two churches, four schools, a golf course, and a community store. When the mine closed in 1950, Dawson's buildings were torn down or relocated, and its residents scattered.

The gravestones are still there, though, and 383 of them bear two specific dates – October 22, 1913, and February 9, 1923 – marking horrific mine disasters. The names reflect the distant lands the workers came from: Italy, Serbia, Czechoslovakia, and the British Isles, among many others. The inscriptions are an elegy to the evanescence of their dreams.

Nevada

Genoa

On a warm weekend afternoon, patrons are sitting at tables outside the Genoa Bar – proclaimed to be Nevada's Oldest Thirst Parlor – and sipping their drinks, as customers have done since 1853, when this false-front brick building was established as Livingston's Exchange.

There's a lot that hasn't changed in a century and a half in this unexpectedly green valley, situated beneath the pine-covered slopes of the Sierra Nevada. The lane that leads four miles from the highway crosses the lazy Carson River, skirts neat pastures, and eventually comes to the crossroads at the middle of the town that was Nevada's first permanent settlement.

On one corner of this crossroads stands Mormon Station State Historic Park, which re-creates the trading post built by pioneers John Reese and Stephen Kinsey in 1851 to supply the stream of gold seekers en route to California. Traditionally, this land was roamed by Washoe Indians, who spent the summers around Lake Tahoe and the autumns gathering pine nuts in the hills to the east. But within a decade the growing wave of settlers – not only Mormons, but others as well – had altered the character of the valley, which became part of Utah Territory.

A score of houses from those early days, often kept private by borders of thick greenery, line the shady streets. Among the oldest is Reese's own residence – the gingerbread-trimmed Pink House from 1853, at the center of town. There's also a cottage named for its proprietor, Mrs. Champagne, and the jaunty brick Victorian Thorington House, whose owner, "Lucky Bill" disproved his name when he was hanged for harboring horse thieves.

In 1854 Governor Brigham Young dispatched Orson Hyde to serve as judge and spiritual leader of the burgeoning community. Hyde plotted the streets and renamed the place Genoa, but within a couple of years he had moved on. Then, in 1857, the Mormon settlers were summoned by Young to defend Salt Lake City against U.S. troops. Of the residents who stayed behind, many lobbied for a separate Nevada Territory, which was finally instituted in 1861, followed by statehood three years later.

Meanwhile, the town thrived as the county seat. Genoa was the first home to the noted *Territorial Enterprise* newspaper and a busy stop on the Pony Express, which carried the mail for a brief but colorful 18 months, until November 1861. Actually the area had

A lovely place for a little rest and relaxation, the spa building at Walley's Hot Springs Resort (opposite) *began with a tent set up near mineral pools where baths went for 50 cents apiece. The local tradition of hospitality got an early start at the Genoa Bar* (above) *and continues with French country cooking at La Ferme Restaurant* (left).

Ghosts linger beyond spiky desert vegetation in Gold Point. (Page 107)

The skiing postman, John "Snowshoe" Thompson, balances in bronze (above) in the center of Genoa. Below: Steam rises over warm mineral pools on a chilly morning.

its own intrepid mail carrier for two decades. From 1856 to 1876, Norwegian-born John "Snowshoe" Thompson delivered letters, small packages, and occasionally a mineral sample twice a month each winter by skiing the mountains between Genoa and Placerville, in California's Gold Country.

Thompson's heroic exploits are memorialized not only in a bronze statue at the town crossroads but also in the exhibits at the Genoa Courthouse Museum. This distinguished two-story brick building replaced the original courthouse that burned in 1910, along with much of downtown. Alas, the county seat shifted to nearby Minden in 1916, and schoolrooms filled the court chambers for the next 40 years. Today the museum houses a blacksmith shop, an old-time post office, and a Victorian-style parlor, kitchen, and nursery, plus the old jail, and a tribute to Nevada's first woman doctor, Genoa's Eliza Cook.

Other aspects of 19th-century life are reflected in the Masonic Lodge, from 1872, whose insignia decorates its Main Street façade; and the simple wood-framed auditorium of the Raycraft Dance Hall, built in 1886 and still a community center. The inviting mineral

pools at Walley's Hot Springs Resort recall the spa and bathhouse established by David and Harriet Walley in 1862 with a ballroom, gardens, and 11 lavish baths.

To be sure, some of the energy went out of Genoa when it lost the county seat. But that didn't stop Lillian Virgin, daughter of a local judge, from organizing a "candy dance" to raise money for streetlights. The tradition she began in 1919 continues to this day, with the September festival pulling in throngs for homemade fudge, a buffet supper, crafts vendors, and the cherished atmosphere of small-town America.

During the rest of the year, visitors find a quiet getaway surrounded by family-owned cattle ranches, though commuters from Carson City are increasingly staking their claims to golf-course real estate. Glider enthusiasts also flock in to take advantage of aeronautical conditions unmatched in the United States, but for fans of terrestrial pleasures, there's a surprising local winery that relies on grapevines particularly suited to Nevada's climate. Virtually across the street from the Genoa Bar, the Tahoe Ridge tasting room offers its own sophisticated and contemporary version of a Nevada "thirst parlor."

The town's august courthouse lost its official role when the county seat moved but later served as a school and then a museum (above). *The Mormon Station State Historic Park* (below) *replicates the town's humble log cabin beginnings.*

Virginia City

Certain towns not only inspire stories, they're also lucky in their storytellers. Take Virginia City. This rough collection of tents and shacks rose to become a wealthy, sophisticated community, with enough minerals in its fabled Comstock Lode to spur the birth of the territory and state of Nevada. The fortunes made and lost here between 1860 and 1880 were enormous, and so were the personalities that passed through, including one Samuel Clemens, who adopted his nom de plume while working for the *Territorial Enterprise* from 1862 to 1863.

Though easterners claim the name Mark Twain harkens back to the writer's days as a Mississippi riverboat pilot, Virginia City inhabitants insist it grew out of his habit of ordering two drinks at Piper's Saloon and chalking it up to his account ("mark twain") on the board. Locals can point to an 1877 newspaper story that supports their claim. But then the Comstock has always loved a good yarn, completely verifiable or not.

Unquestionably, the basic facts of the town add up to an outsize saga. A few prospectors on their way to the California Gold Rush had noticed promising flecks of ore in the area, but not until 1859 did miners find piles of the prized dust at a place they called Gold Hill.

Word spread fast, and as more and more men joined in the "rush to Washoe" (in the words of a popular slogan), two miners were fast-talked into sharing their lucrative claim with a blustery interloper called Henry Comstock. Along with gold, the trio found a gray-blue sludge and cursed it for making their work more difficult – until an assay revealed that the material was

The phenomenal riches of the Comstock Lode created the boisterous boomtown of Virginia City (right) and turned it into a cosmopolitan metropolis of more than 25,000, before the mines went bust.

marvelously pure silver. Some $700 million in ore would make Virginia City world famous.

The Comstock Lode also caught the attention interest of the U.S. Government, which needed funds to wage the Civil War. In 1861 Congress created a separate Nevada Territory out of Utah's domain and welcomed it as a state in 1864.

Meanwhile the daily life of Virginia City – named by a tipsy miner after his home state – was chronicled not only by Twain but also by a handful of other talented writers, including Dan DeQuille and Alf Doten, who sometimes let their imaginations supply colorful details. They had great material to work with. By the mid-1860s small mine claims and companies were being squeezed out by the ruthless Bank Crowd, headed by William Ralston and William Sharon. The town boomed with the arrival of the Virginia & Truckee Railroad in 1868. Then in 1873, just as it seemed that the silver might be petering out, a quartet of partners labeled the Big Four – John Mackay, James Fair, James Flood, and William O'Brien – found the Big Bonanza. With this deep vein of silver, Virginia City rebounded. When a cataclysmic fire in 1875 wiped out two-thirds of its businesses, residents rebuilt within months.

The late-19th-century penchant for ostentation is reflected in the decorative cream-and-white façade of the Storey County Courthouse (left) with a silver Justice, who may have watched accounts as well as her scales; the structure's side wall is plainer brick. In 1876 St. Mary's in the Mountains – the "Bonanza Church" – was built in grand style (below), with redwood arches and pews, after an earlier sanctuary was lost to fire. Rocking chairs set a sedentary 19th-century pace in a cottage at Edith Palmer's Country Inn (opposite left), a small collection of restored houses and an old cider factory.

None of this feels like distant history when you stroll through the town, whose tiers of narrow streets cling to a hillside honeycombed by dozens of mine shafts and tunnels. Turn-of-the-century buildings line C Street, and castle-like mansions and grand mine offices dot the residential areas. Mark Twain's desk presides over a corner of the jumbled basement of the Territorial Enterprise Museum. And several times a day the steam locomotive of the V & T Railroad chugs to Gold Hill and back, past abandoned mine entrances, sagebrush hills, and gray piles of ore tailings. The elaborate courthouse, built in 1876 with a silver statue of an all-seeing Justice, still hosts courtroom dramas, while the soaring red steeple of St. Mary's in the Mountains, another landmark built in the same year, continues to beckon Catholic worshipers.

There are nowhere near the 110 saloons that catered to Virginia City's peak population of almost 30,000, but half a dozen atmospheric drinking establishments take you back to the early days. Step inside, and you'll see gas-style lamps, antique back bars, sepia photos, even a walk-in vault, along with deer heads, assorted trophy undergarments, and the latest poker slot machines.

Behind its red-and-yellow façade, Piper's Opera House provided entertainment beginning in 1878 – from boxing matches to star turns by Lillie Langtry – for just

50 cents in the gallery, $15 for a premium box. Today you can enjoy theatrical fare on its raked stage and savor a libation at a newly restored corner saloon.

Almost everyone in Virginia City has a story. Owners of the town's beautifully renovated bed-and-breakfasts will regale you with tales of the original residents. And the huge three-story Fourth Ward School, now a lively museum, includes an authentic classroom

*T*he Italianate style of the Piper-Beebe House (above), which was owned in the 1950s by the journalists who revived the Territorial Enterprise, *features ornamental details heightened by an elaborate paint scheme.*

A stroll down historic "C" Street (above) transports visitors to the late 1800s. Much of downtown succumbed to a devastating fire in 1875, but within months Virginia City had put up brick-fronted stores, with arcades and balconies, which now house shops, cafés, and saloons.

as well as exhibits on the community's varied citizens: miners who earned a whopping $4 a day, seamstresses who re-created the latest Paris fashions; speculators, inventors, shopkeepers, and prostitutes.

Of course, the boom times didn't last. By the 1880s, the rich ore veins had been played out, and people began drifting away. Over the next decades, properties were abandoned, or families sometimes bought two adjacent houses, one to live in, and one to burn for firewood.

New technology kept the mines limping along until World War II finished them off. But within a few years, outsiders began to rediscover Virginia City, including journalist Lucius Beebe and his partner, Charles Clegg,

The town's most famous chronicler, Mark Twain, came here in 1862 and worked for the Territorial Enterprise. *The museum devoted to that newspaper* (above) *preserves his desk* (opposite below) *amid other artifacts.* Right: *A gambler tries for a modern bonanza at the Mark Twain Saloon.*

who resuscitated the *Territorial Enterprise* in 1952 and made it a weekly success during their nine-year tenure. Yet it took another *Bonanza* to really turn things around. The television series that ran from 1959 to 1973 depicted the Cartwright family's forays to a Virginia City that hardly resembled the actual town but whose name unquestionably drew tourists.

Decades later visitors come to tramp the boardwalk, take a mine tour, sip a beer, and listen to tales of those who struck it unbelievably rich. If they look for silver, they'll find it, too, in the full moon that rises over Six-Mile Canyon and blankets the forbidding hills with a luminous sheen.

Winnemucca

Founded as a provisioning stop for travelers heading west, Winnemucca's downtown (above) *still has the feel of a crossroads community. The legacy of the region's numerous Basque sheepherders lives on* (opposite, top to bottom) *in the historic Winnemucca Hotel bar, the Martin Hotel dining room, and the annual Basque Festival.*

AT MEALTIMES THE long tables of the Martin Hotel's dining room are crowded with friends and strangers. Boys in cowboy hats, girls in tank tops, grandparents, parents, and children all sit elbow to elbow and share the dishes of a bountiful Basque feast: soup to start; green salad; stew or chicken and rice; side dishes of corn, French fries, and vegetables; entrees of lamb chops, pork, or steak; with bread pudding for dessert.

Lunches and dinners in this white clapboard building, which dates from around 1913, recall the days when it was a hostelry for immigrant sheepherders, and Railroad Avenue was a busy street lined with shops, saloons, and hotels, like the false-front Shone House

around the corner. On the walls of the Martin Hotel's bar, turn-of-the-century photos, maps, and memorabilia – including decades-old records of annual deer-hunting competitions – bring whoops of recognition from longtime patrons and returning friends.

The town actually got its start about seven blocks away, close to the Humboldt River that curves and bends under a modern highway. In 1860, a Gallic trader set up shop to supply wagon trains making the trek west, and the place became known as French Ford. By 1863 the Winnemucca Hotel had gone up nearby; it remains the town's oldest structure, renting a few rooms, serving meals in the rear dining room, and

Winnemucca family tell how the colorful bandit camped in the willows on their land while he planned the robbery that would net him $32,000.

Winnemucca's historic buildings reflect the town's development – a school in 1916, the elegant courthouse in 1921, early boarding houses, a motor court, and gracious dwellings, some of which are still visible on the tree-lined avenues. One Gothic Revival house, built by a railroad agent in 1874 and now used by a surveying company, has gingerbread trim on its red, yellow, and blue façade, while a spacious 1912 bungalow serves as the Winnemucca Fine Arts Gallery.

A few turn-of-the-century structures have been moved to the grounds of the Humboldt Museum, including an 1899 Queen Anne Victorian and the 1907 Episcopal church that first displayed the institution's

pouring drinks in front, where a carved wooden back bar adds period atmosphere.

Five years later, when the Central Pacific Railroad arrived, the town's center shifted nearer to the depot, and its name was changed to Winnemucca, to honor a noted Paiute Indian chief. Surrounded by cattle and sheep operations, the community grew, and commercial buildings along Bridge Street eventually connected the river town with the rail town. In 1886, the enterprising George Nixon, destined to be a state senator, built his First National Bank in the middle of the two parts of the settlement, where it became a target for Butch Cassidy in 1900. Stories passed down in one

No rooms are available at this turn-of-the-century inn in tiny Paradise Valley (above), but the old farming and ranching community still conveys a welcoming air to exploring daytrippers.

collections. Today, though, the museum has a fine brick home that showcases Ice Age mammoth bones, artifacts from Winnemucca's now-vanished Chinatown, a dozen vintage cars, a Victorian parlor from nearby Paradise Valley, and an exhibit on Sarah Winnemucca, daughter of the town's namesake and an early advocate for Native American causes.

The little community of Paradise Valley, 35 miles north of Winnemucca, seems not to have changed

much at all. Established in 1863, it remains a quiet crossroads amid bucolic pastures. A general store, a wooden water tower, a saloon, a few antique residences, and a shuttered hotel are all that's left of the village that once provided produce and supplies for area ranches and mines.

Winnemucca itself has tried to stride a fine line between past and present. Its main street is a busy thoroughfare with motels and casinos, but the town also

remains a center for northern Nevada ranches. Regional Western history and lifestyle is honored in the visitors' center, and at the center's Buckaroo Hall of Fame, where the achievements of noted cowboys are commemorated in words, photos, saddles, and other gear.

Beyond the ranches are ore-rich hills that have governed the ups and downs of Winnemucca's mining industry over the years. Gold mining is once again on the upswing, attracting workers who have swelled the population to 7,000. But ask anyone, and they'll tell you that the spirit of community runs as deep among newcomers as fifth-generation residents.

Here festivals invariably bring out the crowds, whether for casual "cruise nights" in 1950s jalopies, hotly contested rodeo competitions, or the colorful Basque gatherings in which dancers, musicians, and cooks take to the streets in an irresistible celebration of Winnemucca's heritage.

Matching towers adorn the Spanish-Mission-style architecture of St. Paul's Catholic Church (above), *constructed in 1924.*

Route 66
THE CLASSIC AMERICAN BYWAY

Seligman, Arizona, seems an unlikely place to attract European tourists, but there they are: a pair of German motorcyclists wearing leather, two French couples, a carful of British sightseers. Foreign languages fill the air at several brightly painted cafés that line the otherwise undistinguished main drag of the town. There is also a steady stream of Americans at the old barbershop and the Snow-Cap Drive-In.

What attracts the visitors is not the food or the scenery or the kitschy trinkets sold in the half-dozen souvenir shops. It's that Seligman lies on Historic Route 66. This little town, in fact, is the epicenter of the movement to recognize – and revive – that fabled highway.

Route 66 – 2,448 miles from Chicago to Los Angeles – officially entered the U.S. highway system in 1926. But great stretches of the road followed long-established east–west trade routes used by Native Americans, trails later followed by Spanish padres and rutted by wagons heading toward California in the late 1800s. During the Depression, thousands of Dust Bowl emigrants followed Route 66 out of Oklahoma to the promise of a brighter future, prompting John Steinbeck famously to call it the "Mother Road" in *The Grapes of Wrath*.

Throughout the 20th century, as Americans embraced automobile travel, Route 66 introduced them to the wonders of the American Southwest. From the car they could admire vistas of buttes, mesas, and cactus-studded deserts extending to the horizon. Red rocks, limitless blue sky, intermittent dashes of greenery, or even a rash of spring wildflowers offered an enticing palette to travelers from gray cities of the East. There was the Painted Desert, with its improbable pink and yellow rock panoramas, and the Petrified Forest, where massive prehistoric logs had been transformed into gold or purple crystalline and agate sculptures.

Route 66 also introduced travelers to the lands of the American Indians and the trading posts where they could find rugs, pottery, and jewelry to take home as mementos of their cross-country journeys.

To serve the travelers, motels, cafés, and souvenir shops popped up, which in turn became symbols of classic roadside architecture and eventually tourist sights in their own right. The neon signs, oddly shaped buildings, symbols of Indians, cowboys, cacti, and animals (from jack

The "Mother Road," Route 66 twists and turns its way through starkly striking hills near Oatman, Arizona (opposite). *The historic 2,448-mile highway carried Okies west in search of work in California and dazzled generations of automobile travelers with unforgettable panoramas. Today when travelers tuck in for the night, the Southwest landscapes have to compete with cable television* (above).

A sign of bygone times, the Route 66 shield on the pavement (below) lets drivers know that they're on the historic road. Here, as in many spots, the highway parallels railroad tracks. A tin lizzie, a pink convertible, and a pair of outdated gas pumps set the scene in front of the Hackberry General Store (right), which is filled with kitschy relics.

Cutouts add to the crowd at The Rusty Bolt and Thunderbird Indian Store (right) in Seligman (opposite above). Thanks to the efforts of the Delgadillo brothers, who had businesses here, the town has become a must-see stop for pilgrims retracing the fabled route.

rabbits to dinosaurs), plus the catchy song "Get Your Kicks on Route 66" and a popular 1960s television series all contributed to the road's mystique.

In the end, the car culture that gave Route 66 its biggest boost helped kill it off. As the new interstate highway system crisscrossed the country, it denied easy access to quirky places and older attractions along the route. Where Route 66 had gone right through the towns, the interstate highways had specific designated exits that hardly encouraged motorists to stop and explore. The journey was faster, seamless…but blander.

In 1984 Williams, Arizona, became the last Route 66 town to be bypassed by the interstate, and it seemed that the story of "America's Main Street" was over. For more than a decade, many of the small communities

along the route, deprived of their economic lifeline, had been dying out. The motels had closed, the cafés were shuttered, the old gas pumps were empty. Seligman, too, was on the verge of becoming a ghost town.

Enter the Delgadillo brothers – Angel, who owns the barbershop and souvenir store, and the late Juan, whose son now runs the Snow-Cap Drive-In. In 1987 they helped to form the Historic Route 66 Association of Arizona, which has worked to preserve the Mother Road. Today maps and guides pinpoint landmarks from one end of Historic Route 66 to the other.

Some of the most evocative spots are in Arizona and New Mexico. Oatman, Arizona, is a ramshackle almost-ghost-town, where wild burros roam the street between staged gunfights. In Kingman the renovated

Once mere necessities, places to stay and eat along Route 66 have turned into mini-destinations. The teepees of the Wigwam Motel (above) in Holbrook often have retro autos parked in front, and the Frontier Café in Truxton (left) still serves a mean lemon meringue pie.

*R*estoration has brought back the sheen to Gallup's El Rancho Hotel (above), where Hollywood celebrities from Spencer Tracy and Katherine Hepburn to Errol Flynn and Kirk Douglas all signed the guest register.

Powerhouse Visitor Center includes a museum devoted to Route 66. The General Store in Hackberry is jammed floor-to-ceiling with books, memorabilia, and tchotchkes stamped with the highway's shield-shaped logo. Route 66 slices through downtown Williams, passing the Santa Fe Railroad depot with the "last stoplight" in front, and continuing into the atmospheric old section of Flagstaff. Farther east, there's Winslow — where a statue immortalizes the Eagles' lyric about "standing on a corner" in the song "Take It Easy" — and Holbrook, with its venerable teepee-shaped accommodations beckoning travelers to stay in the Wigwam Motel.

Over the New Mexico border, murals and memorabilia in Gallup's still thriving El Rancho Hotel recalls the movie greats who stayed there, while in Grants the iconic neon signs tend to denote fading motels and cafés. Route 66 also runs along the edge of Albuquerque's artsy Old Town, in front of the tiled façade of the historic KiMo Theatre.

The towns evoke an America of a half-century ago, but seen now with a mix of irony and nostalgia. Perhaps the view is less complicated on sections of Route 66 that slice through the middle of nowhere, where clumps of grass break up the blacktop and rough buttes punctuate the horizon. There the landscape — and the possibilities of the future — still seem unbelievably vast.

New Mexico

Chimayó, Las Trampas & Truchas

*I*n *Taos strings of bright* ristras *tempt travelers to take home the* chili *flavor of New Mexico* (page 127).

*B*uilt in response to a miraculous *occurrence, the Santuario de Chimayó* (opposite) *includes a courtyard cemetery inside its low wall. The subtle earth tones of the exterior hardly hint at the brilliant religious art inside* (below)*, which includes works by José and Miguel Aragón and Molleno, the "Chili Painter".*

IN A SIDE chapel of the Santuario de Chimayó, rows of crutches hang on the wall, testaments to the belief in the healing power of the soil in a shallow pit in an adjoining chamber. An exuberant outpouring of religious art brightens the main sanctuary, from the carved crucifix known as the Lord of Esquipulas above the altar to five gorgeous reredos depicting saints surrounded by painted columns and decorative arches. The reredos were painted between 1820 and 1850, a few decades after this adobe chapel was begun, in 1813, by Don Bernardo Abeyta, to honor the miracle that is said to have taken place at Chimayó.

Abeyta was doing penance in the hills nearby, one legend goes, when he saw a light shining from the ground. Digging, he found the crucifix and brought it back to Chimayó, where he told his priest about it. They carried the cross in a procession to Santa Cruz, but the next morning it was gone – returned to the spot where Abeyta had found it. Three times this happened, until it was clear that the crucifix was meant to stay where it had been discovered.

Pilgrims have been coming to this sanctuary ever since, especially around Easter, when thousands arrive on foot or on their knees. Native Americans, too, claim

*G*rateful pilgrims to Chimayó
have left their crucifixes and
crutches in a chamber beside the
main sanctuary (top). *Aztec dancers
(above and right)* perform their
ceremonies at an altar outside.

A tiny belfry denotes a private oratory in one of the adobes that surround the Plaza del Cerro (above), which retains the form of a Hispanic village of the 1700s. Right: the hacienda-style dining room of the Rancho de Chimayó.

that the Chimayó area is sacred, and Aztec dancers travel here several times a year for ceremonies that combine traditional and Catholic beliefs.

Despite the constant stream of outsiders, Chimayó retains the air of a secluded Hispanic village. Many families trace their roots to Spanish settlers who moved into the area in the early 1700s. Their stories are celebrated in a small museum that occupies the adobe homestead of the Ortegas, who, like the Trujillos and the Martinez clan, go back generations here and are famous for the weaving skills passed from parent to child.

The original village centered around the Plaza del Cerro, which was bordered by a nearly contiguous set of low adobe houses and criss-crossed by an *acequia*, a traditional irrigation ditch. Water still flows through the old plaza, though the square itself is overgrown, and

a road bisects what was once a fortified enclosure. The buildings are in various states of repair. One bed-and-breakfast brings life to several restored dwellings; a few doors down, the old post office is now an architect's office. But across the way a private chapel dedicated to San Buenaventura stands empty and forlorn.

The surrounding *ranchito* fields, however, are still used for grazing small herds of cattle. And two haciendas belonging to the Jaramillo family have been preserved – one as a homestyle restaurant and another as a tranquil bed-and-breakfast, with guest rooms arranged around a private courtyard.

Chimayó is just one of several Hispanic communities that sprang up along the "high road" to Taos. Las Trampas, roughly 15 miles north, was established in 1751 and nine years later got its own adobe church with two bell towers.

Closer to Chimayó, other villages are known for traditional crafts, like Cordova, where families of wood carvers made their homes in a quiet valley.

Truchas stands on more mountainous ground, surrounded by slopes of aspen and pine. The village has a general store, a yarn-filled workshop where a weaver carries on the work his father did, and a tiny church dating to 1784, now open only on special occasions. Bells and banners along the road also announce a dozen or so art galleries in old barns and residences, former churches, and farm buildings. In Truchas, it seems, a community of serious painters, metal sculptors, photographers, and craftsmen have declared their faith in the power of art.

A highlight of the "high road" to Taos, the adobe San José de Gracia (above) was built in 1760, after a dozen families received a land grant to settle Las Trampas. Traditional and modern art are intertwined in these villages. A contemporary San Rafael (right), with his stick and fish, occupies a courtyard of a restaurant. In Truchas a deconsecrated church houses a contemporary gallery (opposite above), while one painter has turned part of his studio into an art-filled café (opposite below left). Not far away, weaver Harry Cordova carries on his craft using shuttles his father made (opposite below right).

Chimayó, Las Trampas & Truchas • 133

Cimarron & Raton

CAPULIN VOLCANO RISES abruptly out of the north-eastern New Mexico plains, a dark 8,182-foot-high cinder cone created during an eruption perhaps 60,000 years ago. A road leads almost to the top, where you can peer into the crater or hike a mile-long trail around the rim. From there, on a clear day, the panorama stretches into Texas, Oklahoma, and Colorado in one direction,

and to New Mexico's jagged Sangre de Cristo Mountains in the other.

What a welcome landmark the volcano must have been for the explorers, soldiers, and traders passing nearby on the Santa Fe Trail. The view hints at the vast, rugged landscape that these early travelers encountered: dry plains through Indian country, tricky Raton Pass, pinon- and juniper-covered mesas. Beyond were unbroken grasslands, like those around the tiny settlement at Cimarron.

It was there that a trader and scout named Lucien Maxwell established the headquarters for his two-million-acre ranch, part of a land grant that dated to 1841. Maxwell had inherited much of the estate from his father-in-law and bought the rest from other heirs. By the 1860s he had thousands of cattle, sheep, and horses, and lucrative fields of hay and other crops.

Maxwell built a large residence and used half of it for a wayside inn with "entertainment," which meant vices

like drinking and gambling. Though his house is gone, other vestiges of the 19th-century village are clustered in an easy-to-explore historic district. The stately sandstone-brick Aztec Grist Mill, from about 1860, is a museum filled with furnishings, clothes, and other relics of 19th-century life. The 1863 stagecoach office, marked "Cimarron Mercantile," houses an artist's studio. But the town's real showpiece is the renovated St. James Hotel, founded as a saloon in 1872 by Henri Lambert, Abraham Lincoln's personal chef. Inside, the rooms memorialize former guests, including Bat Masterson, Jesse James, and Ned Buntline. They must have

*T*he sleepy town of Cimarron (above) *was the heart of a two-million-acre ranch owned by Lucien Maxwell in the 1860s. Part of his enormous estate is now a private hunting preserve with a thriving herd of elk* (right).

A repository of Cimarron's past, today the Aztec Grist Mill (top) is a town museum. The St. James Hotel lobby (above), filled with 19th-century memorabilia, accommodates 21st-century guests. Right: Whimsically attired Maxwell memorial.

enjoyed a wild time, judging from the bullet holes in the dining-room ceiling.

When gold was found on nearby Baldy Mountain, Maxwell first increased his fortune by leasing land to miners, then sold out to British speculators in 1870. But disputes and questions about the title lingered, erupting in 1875 in a period of violence called the Colfax County War.

Calm had returned by 1906, when a spur line of the railroad shifted the center of Cimarron nearer to its new depot, where there are now a half-dozen art galleries and boutiques as well as a retro soda fountain. The surrounding plains, though, evoke the old Maxwell Land Grant with gigantic estates like Ted Turner's Vermejo Park and the nearly 128,000 acres of Philmont Scout Ranch, donated to the Boy Scouts of America by oilman Waite Phillips.

The railroad also gave birth, in 1880, to Raton, about 35 miles away. The heady expectations of the town's early entrepreneurs are evident in the turn-of-the-century architecture along First Street, opposite the

train station still used by Amtrak passengers. There's the three-story sandstone-brick former Palace Hotel, and the eye-catching yellow-and-blue façade of Marchiondo's Golden Rule and New York Store. One cast-iron building – currently housing an appliance center – has a silver façade with garlands in dark red. Saloons have been turned into antique stores, the Wells Fargo Office into an arts center.

Raton prospered and grew in the early 1900s, as coal mines were developed and the population increased. The business district expanded with commercial blocks that are home to long-standing and sometimes surprising local enterprises. Step into the 1918 building that includes Solano's Boot and Western Wear, and you'll find a "cowboy hat cemetery" with headgear donated by three decades of loyal customers. The neoclassical library, built in 1917, displays a remarkable collection of paintings by Southwestern artists among its stacks of books.

Although locals bemoan the closing of the mines a half-dozen years ago, one institution has been revived

With decorative pilasters, pediments, and cornices and several creative coats of paint, the façades of Raton's First Street (above) *carry on the look of the late 1800s. At the turn of the century these buildings were bustling grocery and dry goods stores, a saloon, and a meeting hall, serving locals and passengers who arrived at the railroad depot across the way, where 60 trains a day passed through.*

with glittering success. The Shuler Theater, built in 1914, was a wreck when Bill Fegan first came with his Kaleidoscope Theater Company in 1963. Volunteers set about repairing the rococo-style opera house, restoring the lobby murals that had been painted by a Works Progress Administration artist in 1934, and gradually refurbishing the entire theater, down to the ornate gold-and-silver plaster proscenium. Today the Shuler is the pride of Raton, and its busy stage is enhanced by the original canvas drop, which celebrates the region's landscape in a hand-painted image of the Palisades of the Cimarron.

The view from the top of Capulin Volcano (right), *an extinct cinder cone, sweeps for miles. Inside the Shuler Theater in Raton, puffy clouds in a blue sky surmount the glittering proscenium with a hand-painted canvas drop* (below). *Volunteers restored the opera house, which hosts a year-long roster of performing arts.*

Las Vegas

THESE DAYS, WHEN the name generally conjures up a glittering, gambling-happy Nevada metropolis, few people realize that for travelers in the mid-1800s Las Vegas – *in New Mexico* – was the place to stop. Especially if you had spent months riding the dusty, difficult, often dangerous trail that led from Missouri to Santa Fe.

Las Vegas ("the meadows") was founded in 1833 by a few Hispanic families who set up a central plaza, dug out *acequias*, traditional irrigation ditches, to water their fields, and soon prospered as freighters, drivers, and merchants supplying the increasing number of traders on the Santa Fe Trail. The streets south of the plaza hint at what the town looked like in those early times, when horse-drawn wagons passed through a corridor of unbroken, flat-roofed, one-room-wide adobes enclosing gardens and courtyards.

Over the next decades the houses took on a more territorial look, using sawn lumber to replace old-style *vigas* and adding porches among other architectural details. Yet Las Vegas remained a homogeneous Hispanic community until the arrival of the railroad, in 1879. Then, suddenly, the town had a second commercial center at the end of the tracks and a flood of workers, entrepreneurs, and opportunists from all over the world.

The newcomers laid out an orderly grid of streets and parks and built Victorian homes that are now restored gems among the town's 900 registered historic structures. Wiley House, for example, has an elegant octagonal tower, while the lavish lavender-toned Fort House was commissioned by a local district attorney out of a residential pattern-book. Saloon owner D. T. Lowry spent his money on a gracious dwelling with pricey curved windows looking out onto the surrounding porch, and regional rail superintendent George Sands lived in an Eastlake beauty with intricately carved details. The railway depot itself was built in Mission Revival style, matching the shady arcades of the Castaneda Hotel next door.

A ceramic wall plaque on the side of an antique store (left) *announces the historic center of Las Vegas. The town's original settlers kept livestock in the plaza and later welcomed weary wagon trains on the Santa Fe Trail. In the wild 1870s vigilantes strung up bandits on a windmill in the square. A bandstand later replaced the gallows. In 1882, entrepreneurs built the stylish Plaza Hotel on the north side* (opposite above) *to house visitors brought by the railroad. Superbly renovated, the hostelry retains its turn-of-the-century appointments in the lobby* (opposite below) *and rooms.*

Old Town Las Vegas went through its own turn-of-the-century building spree. Neat brick storefronts topped by fancy cornices and sporting colorful painted trim went up on Bridge Street, where it's still easy to find the signs of a bygone era. The names "Stern and Nahm" above a set of tall windows recall a dry-goods store from 1885, while "E. Romero Hose and Fire Company" on a wide entryway proclaims the building's use in 1919. On the plaza one impressive Italianate façade conveyed the solidity and wealth of a bank, while the three-story Plaza Hotel opened its oversized doors in 1882 to reveal a lobby illuminated by a gleaming chandelier.

A railway spur line carried visitors to the hot springs at Montezuma, just five miles away, where they could stay in a castle-like hotel designed by famed Chicago architects Daniel Burnham and John Root in 1880. Closed in 1903 and sold and resold several times, the monumental building now houses students of the United World College.

With the railway came a contingent of notorious Old West characters. Doc Holliday ran a saloon in Las Vegas, and Bat Masterson conducted business in town.

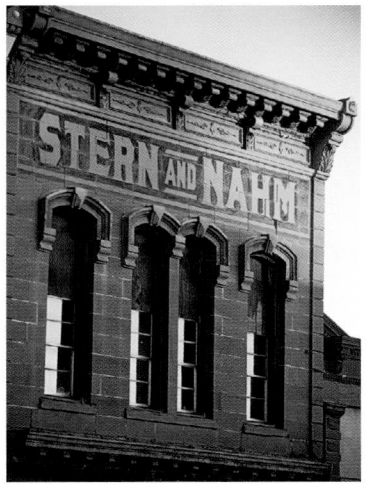

Even Jesse James and Billy the Kid are said to have met, perhaps over a game of cards, at the Old Adobe Hotel. That's not as farfetched as it sounds. Las Vegas was a known William Bonney hangout, and the hotel was owned by a longtime James acquaintance. It's entirely possible the two famous outlaws crossed paths here.

Meanwhile, lesser criminals and cowboys lived it up in the dancehalls and saloons. Vicente Silva ran a group of 40 bandits from his Cantina Imperial – open 24 hours a day – on the south side of the plaza, until his own men murdered him. To keep order, the town organized vigilantes, who frequently resorted to a "hanging windmill" on the plaza.

When the call went out in 1898 to serve in the Spanish–American War, the New Mexico Territory sent a huge contingent. A year later the Rough Riders chose Las Vegas for their reunion, the first of yearly get-togethers that continued until 1968.

By the 1970s the prosperous times had been over for nearly 50 years. Many of the architectural treasures on

Bridge Street were empty or dilapidated, though local preservationists had begun to raise the alarm. In 1983, the sale and renovation of the Plaza Hotel helped spark a wider movement to restore the historic buildings.

Once again old storefronts are bright with pink, yellow, or green detailing, and their displays offer a tempting array of jewelry, fashionable clothing, books and music, and Southwestern arts and crafts. You can savor a dish of ice cream among glass display cases in the corner drugstore, or sip a drink in the convivial saloon in the Plaza Hotel. There, through the windows, on a warm Thursday evening, say, you have a good view of the members of a local salsa club crowding the gazebo in the center of the plaza and dancing the night away.

Cafés and shops line Bridge Street (above) *where the commercial past lingers in old street signs* (opposite top). *After-dark options include a drink at Byron T's Saloon* (opposite center) *or sometimes salsa dancing in the plaza* (opposite below).

Mesilla

With a colorful swirl of skirts, a Mexican folkloric group (above) performs as part of the Cinco de Mayo celebration in Mesilla's plaza, a gathering spot since the place was founded. In 1871 political marches around the square turned violent when rival factions met in front of what's now the Mesilla Book Center (opposite above). The adobe structures here often had defensive brick parapets. Clay luminarias top the walls of La Posta Restaurant (opposite below), where the doors and windows are trimmed in traditional blue.

THE BAND CAME OUT in front of the gazebo at the center of Mesilla's plaza. It was the end of Cinco de Mayo, and the food and trinket booths were packing up. But the party wasn't over yet. As the musicians began playing, couples eased out onto the grass and into a familiar polka. An old cowboy with a lady in trim blouse and jeans, a well-dressed couple spinning forward and back, a baby boomer with a graying pony-tail and a younger woman in a miniskirt – they all knew the steps to the dance that melded oompah rhythms with Mexican verve. When that song finished, the dancers segued seamlessly into a sedate *cumbia*.

The scene had an old-time village feel, but then Mesilla is an old-time village. Its location near New Mexico's southern border – along old trails that linked Santa Fe and Chihuahua and San Diego and San Antonio

– helped give the settlement its start in the mid-1800s as a hub for trade and transportation. But it wasn't really until the end of the Mexican War, in 1848, that a permanent community grew up here. In that year, the treaty of Guadalupe Hidalgo set the boundary of the United States at the Rio Grande River. Unfortunately, the maps dis-agreed as to where exactly the river was – a situation that worsened when the river changed its course.

By 1850 Mesilla had 600 residents, who were claimed as citizens by both the United States and Mexico. Three years later, when the Gadsden Purchase made Mesillans U.S. citizens for good, the population had quadrupled. With Apache raids a constant worry, the villagers built their houses to resemble little forts, with parapets for defense and narrow double-gated pas-sageways that could be barred against intruders. The

They say lovers' ghosts haunt the Double Eagle (above), whose hand-carved Eastlake-style bar stretches for 30 feet under Baccarat crystal chandeliers. Originally a magnificent dwelling, the structure was used for hay storage before being gorgeously restored.

presence of Fort Fillmore also added a sense of security, both for the town and for the stagecoach lines that began to carry people and mail to the West Coast in the 1850s. A decade later, during the Civil War, Confederate troops were headquartered in Mesilla, which temporarily became the territorial capital, until Union soldiers pushed the Rebels out of New Mexico.

The buildings around the plaza reflect the traditional lifestyle of those times. San Albino Church has been the religious center of the community since the mid-1800s, calling the faithful with bells rung by the

same family for three generations. Its current brick edifice, which dates from 1907, was built above and around an earlier adobe chapel.

The buildings at the opposite end of the plaza, known as the "transportation block," had entries and court-yards large enough to accommodate wagons and horses. For passengers, the complex conveniently included a saloon, a tradition that continues unbroken in the lively El Patio Bar.

Down the block, another stage stop – owned for a while by Sam Bean and his famous brother, Roy – was

turned into a hotel in the 1870s before becoming the atmospheric La Posta Restaurant 70 years ago.

The east and west sides of the plaza have long been a mix of homes and businesses. The oldest dwelling, constructed in the late 1840s, is said to harbor the ghosts of the original household's son and the maid he loved – both killed by his mother, who disapproved of the match. The sumptuous residence, which served as the governor's mansion during the Civil War, was restored to its earlier splendor about 30 years ago, when it opened as the Double Eagle, with an elaborate bar,

crystal chandeliers in the entry, and an 18-carat gold ceiling in the formal dining room.

Across the way, the bookstore, built in the 1850s and owned by Joseph Reynolds and J. Edgar Griggs (who also operated the general store next door) retains its old-time architectural details, including fireplaces, vigas, and latilla ceilings. It was just outside the bookstore, on August 27, 1871, that a bizarre political fracas took place, when both Democrats and Republicans decided to rally on the plaza. Marching from opposite ends, the two parties met in a violent confrontation. Before it was over, nine men were

Holiday lights brighten the plaza (above), *with San Albino Church anchoring the north end. The brick sanctuary* (opposite above), *with its three named bells, was dedicated to a saintly protector of the* acequias *that watered communal fields.*

dead and scores injured. Twenty years later, Reynolds and Griggs added the cast-iron façade – ordered out of the Sears catalog – to the general store that bears their names.

The shop at the southeast corner of the plaza has its own colorful story. In 1881 it was the county courthouse where William Bonney, alias Billy the Kid, was convicted of murder and sentenced to hang. Bonney escaped from custody, however, and instead died at Pat Garrett's hand.

Not long after, the railway bypassed Mesilla in favor of Las Cruces, four miles away, and the village lost its importance. But more than a century later, art galleries and boutiques fill buildings that have been listed on the historic register, and water flows in the 150-year-old *acequia* that used to water residents' fields. For the last 80 years those acres have been transformed into pecan orchards, whose cycles of flower, fruit, and harvest follow their own time-honored rhythms.

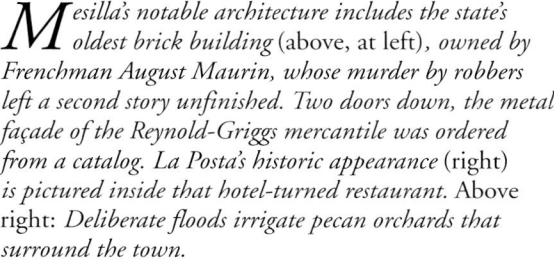

*M*esilla's notable architecture includes the state's oldest brick building (above, at left), owned by Frenchman August Maurin, whose murder by robbers left a second story unfinished. Two doors down, the metal façade of the Reynold-Griggs mercantile was ordered from a catalog. La Posta's historic appearance (right) is pictured inside that hotel-turned restaurant. Above right: Deliberate floods irrigate pecan orchards that surround the town.

Taos

Dovecotes on stilts lie just inside the gates of Mabel Dodge Luhan's house (opposite), constructed by the wealthy socialite with her Taos Indian husband, Tony. Among the writers and artists she hosted were D. H. Lawrence and Georgia O'Keeffe, who famously painted the church at Ranchos de Taos (above), which was begun in the late 1700s.

IT'S AN ART lover's feast. Dozens of galleries line the streets of Taos, filled with elegant Native American rugs and pottery, rustic wooden *santos* fashioned by Hispanic carvers, and luminous paintings by Anglo artists of the Taos School – masterworks of the three cultures that have defined this timeless place.

Here, in a high valley between the Sangre de Cristo Mountains and the Rio Grande, pueblo dwellers made a home possibly a thousand years ago. Taos Pueblo still looks much as it did when conquistadors passed through in the 16th century: two sets of boxy adobe dwellings without electricity or running water, stacked in two- or three-story tiers on a broad plaza divided by Red Willow Creek.

San Geronimo Church, built in 1850, stands at the entrance to the pueblo, next to the cemetery and the ruins of the mission established by the Spanish in 1619. Decades of harsh treatment at European hands led to the successful Pueblo Revolt, which erupted here in 1680 and quickly spread.

For two decades the Spanish retreated. But in the early 1700s they regained control of Taos and built a plaza, ranchos, and haciendas on land grants issued by the king of Spain. They dedicated a church to San Francisco de Asís at Ranchos de Taos and decorated the interior with brilliant *retablos* of saints and mystical symbols. By then other outsiders were also drifting into the area, first French fur traders and later

mountain men who traded pelts in the Taos plaza during yearly rendezvous.

The Hacienda de los Martinez recreates the lifestyle of a well-off Hispanic *vecino*, or citizen, of the early 1800s. Its simply furnished adobe rooms enclose two *placitas*, or courtyards, where family members and live-stock would be safe from Indian attack. The hacienda also incorporated workshops for processing the wool that underpinned the early economy.

For a traditional Anglo residence, there's Kit Carson's house, though the intrepid trapper, guide, Indian agent, and Army officer was anything but a traditional Anglo. Carson moved to Taos in 1826, when the town belonged to the Mexican Republic; he and his Hispanic wife, Josefa, would raise eight children there before his death in 1868.

When the Mexican–American War broke out in 1846, the U.S. army occupied New Mexico, and Charles Bent, a well-known trader on the Santa Fe Trail, was appointed governor. Resentment of the new regime ran deep, however, and in 1847 a mob killed Bent in his Taos home. Troops retaliated brutally, storming the pueblo, killing 150 Indians, and

As a mountain man and trapper, Kit Carson came to Taos to trade his pelts in the 1820s. In 1843, when he married Maria Josefa Jaramillo, his wedding gift to her was a simple one-story adobe with viga-and-latilla ceilings (opposite) just east of the plaza, and they lived there off and on for 25 years. Above: Red Willow Creek flows through the center of Taos Pueblo, providing drinking water for the village, whose age-old dwellings get by without electricity. In 1680 this was the center of a revolt that drove out the Spanish till the early 1700s. After the conquerors returned to the area, they built San Francisco de Asís. The church's magnificent retablo (left) includes brilliant folk paintings from the 1820s, which surround more sober religious art that may have come from Mexico or Spain.

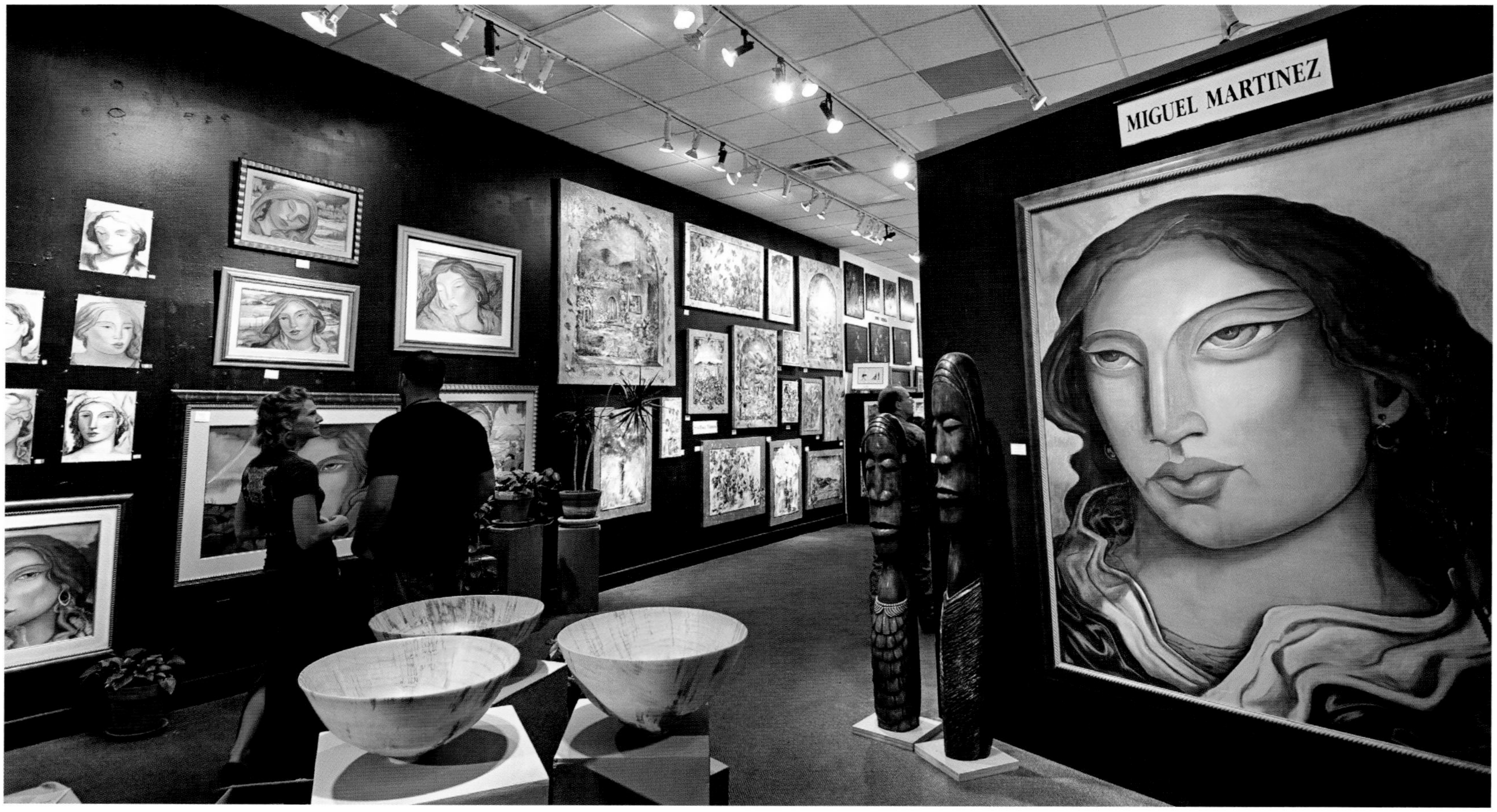
MIGUEL MARTINEZ

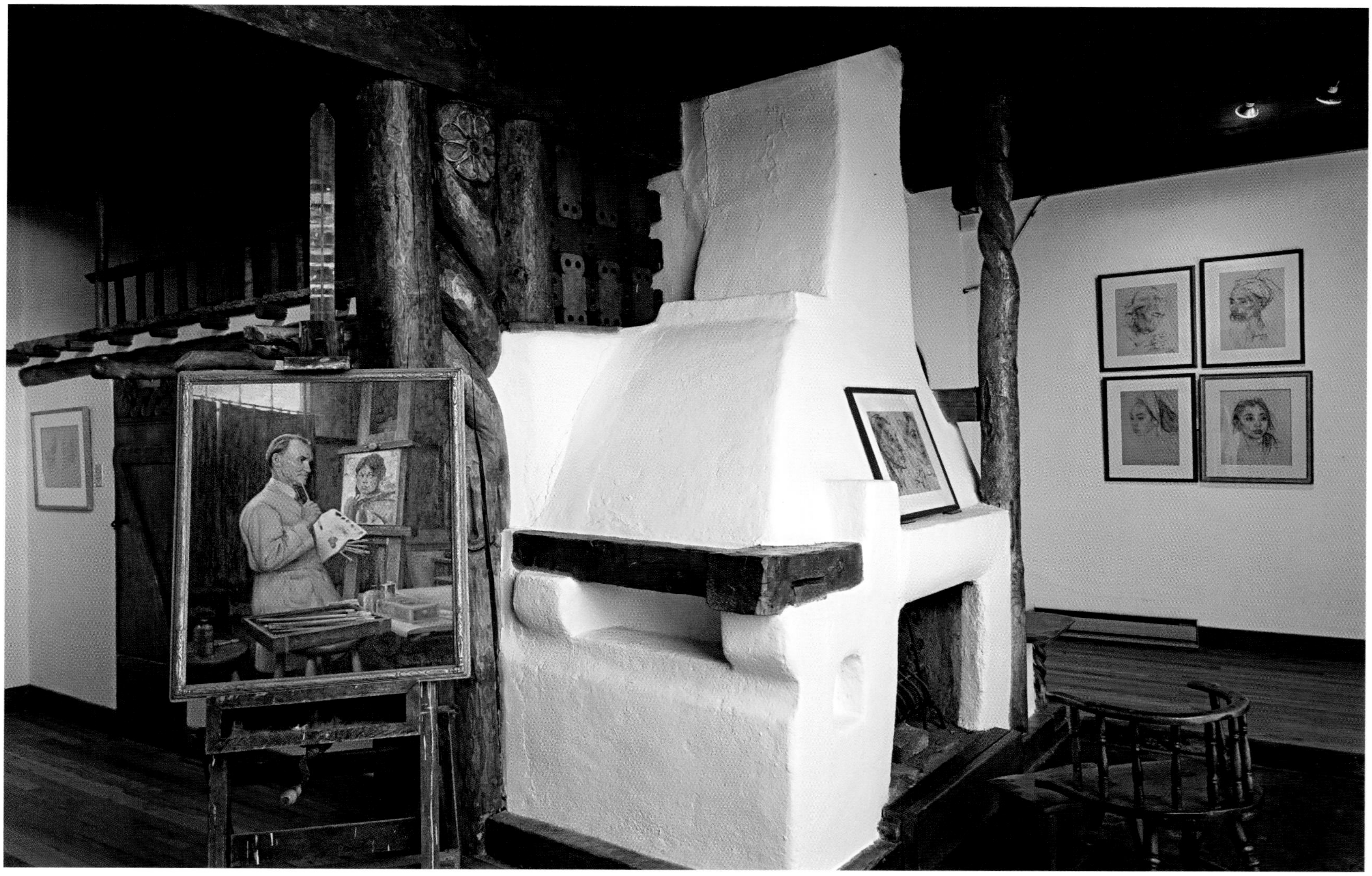

A pow-wow at Taos Pueblo *brings out dancers in full regalia* (right) *and racks of hand-woven work* (above). *Orlando's New Mexican-style cuisine attracts a crowd to its brightly hued cottage setting* (below).

*N*icolas Fechin turned his *studio* (opposite below) *and home into sculpture with carved pillars, furniture, and other details. The work of contemporary painters fills the Michael McCormick Gallery* (opposite above), *one of a dozen in Taos.*

razing the original mission church. A year later Taos permanently was joined to the United States, following the Treaty of Guadalupe Hildalgo. Yet the town retained its pueblo-style architecture and its ties to Native American and Hispanic cultures, creating a unique atmosphere that attracted a different kind of resident.

In 1898 two East Coast painters, Ernest Blumenschein and Bert Phillips, were sketching their way through the Southwest when their wagon broke down 20 miles from Taos. The setting proved irresistible. A two-month sojourn turned into a lifetime for Phillips, who married Rose Martin, the sister of the local doctor; Blumenschein returned east, but he came back often over the next two decades, until he, too, moved to town for good.

In 1915 the pair, joined by Joseph Sharp, Oscar Berninghaus, Irving Couse, and Herbert "Buck" Dunton, formed the Taos Society of Artists in a side room of Doc Martin's house. Their depictions of pueblos, plazas, adobes, and light-filled landscapes came to define the quintessential Southwest and soon attracted other painters as well as literary figures.

Mabel Dodge, for example, had been a prominent hostess to writers and political thinkers in New York and Europe. When she decided to rebuild an adobe house in Taos in 1918, and married Native American Tony Luhan, she invited D. H. Lawrence – who painted the windows of her second-floor bathroom – as well as Aldous Huxley and Willa Cather. Georgia O'Keeffe and Ansel Adams also paid visits; the images they made of the church at Ranchos de Taos are now part of New Mexico's iconography.

Decades later art is all-pervasive in Taos. Russian-born artist Nikolai Fechin, another of Mabel Dodge

*K*eeping up appearances in the Taos Pueblo (opposite) *calls for refurbishing the adobe exteriors, which may go back 1,000 years. The softened boxy shape of the homes and the customary blue doors and window frames set the architectural style throughout town. On Ledoux Street* (below), *a gallery has introduced its own oversized lighthearted touches, and a shop on the main street places stout pots as wall decorations above a statue of the Virgin in a tiled niche* (right).

Luhan's guests, built a house and studio in the growing art colony, adding hand-carved columns, furniture, and doors that turned it into a masterpiece in itself. Blumenschein's house is another museum; Dodge Luhan's restored home is a conference center and hotel; and nine of D. H. Lawrence's "erotic" paintings have been installed at the Hotel La Fonda de Taos. Murals with judicial themes, painted by several Taos Society artists in the 1930s, add artful drama to the county courthouse, while other works are on exhibit in the Harwood Museum of Art. Magnificent Native American textiles, pottery, jewelry, and Hispanic carvings fill the Millicent Rogers Museum, based on the collection of the New York heiress who made Taos her home in the late 1940s.

Just as Taos's artistic tradition is carried on by a thriving community of contemporary painters, sculptors, textile artists, and craftspeople, the landscape that stirred the artists continues to work its magic in other ways, inspiring those who raft the Rio Grande, bike the mountain trails, or ski Taos's challenging snowy slopes.

Petroglyphs, Pueblos, Trading Posts, and Pow-wows
EXPLORING THE NATIVE AMERICAN SOUTHWEST

Tucked below a rocky overhang in a canyon in southwestern Colorado, Mesa Verde's Cliff Palace is at once eerie and familiar. Swifts glide in front of the magnificent complex, whose ancient sandstone blocks outline towers, rooms, and round underground spaces called kivas. Even in its partly ruined state, this cliff dwelling is clearly recognizable as an apartment house of sorts, where it's easy to imagine men, women, and children doing chores, cooking, eating, and sleeping.

Roughly 100 people lived in the 150-room Cliff Palace, which was built from *c.* 1190 through 1280 C.E. Along with 30 "living rooms" were dozens of storerooms and more than 20 kivas for ceremonies, as well as plazas and open work areas. Fields of corn, squash, and beans occupied the mesa tops, yet it all was abandoned – perhaps because of drought, though disease and warfare are also possibilities. By 1300 Cliff Palace's inhabitants, often called Ancestral Puebloans or Anasazi, were gone.

Mesa Verde's largest cliff dwelling, Cliff Palace is only one among 600 known dwellings in this World Heritage Site, which includes 4,500 archaeological sites in total. Spruce Tree House, with 114 rooms, is actually the best preserved, but you can also visit Balcony House, Square Tower House, Step House, Long House, and the remains of earlier settlements.

You're likely to have company. Mesa Verde has drawn visitors since 1888, when a pair of local ranchers spotted some ruins while herding cattle. Before long they were showing the way to other curious travelers, and by 1906 the place was popular enough – and vulnerable to the "collection" of artifacts – that it was protected as a national park.

The Southwest offers widespread opportunities to explore Native Americans' varied cultures and heritages. Their ways of life, their arts, and their gatherings provide glimpses into the beliefs that reflect a long, deep connection with this stunning landscape.

People have inhabited the Southwest for at least 11,500 years, though archaeological evidence seems to be pushing that date back further and further. Over the centuries, hunting with spear and atlatl gave way to using bow and arrow, and gathering seeds and tubers evolved into planting corn.

The view of Mesa Verde's Cliff Palace (opposite) *has captivated visitors for more than a century, puzzling them with the mystery of where the Anasazi – the people who lived here until about 1280 C.E. – went when they abandoned it. The 150 rooms included living and working areas, storage spaces, and ceremonial kivas reached by ladders* (below). *Cliff dwellings abound in the Four Corners area; there are hundreds within Mesa Verde National Park alone. As for the Anasazi, archaeologists now believe they are tied to the modern Hopi and Pueblo tribes.*

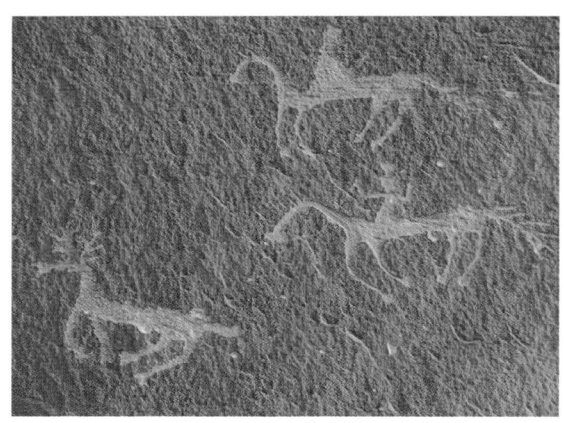

The sandstone walls of Canyon de Chelly (opposite) harbor Anasazi cliff dwellings and later Navajo petroglyphs showing men on horseback (above right). Near Lake Powell earlier rock art shows stylized figures (above center), while kiva murals (above) are a highlight at 14th-century Coronado State Monument. Anasazi connections reached outward from the curving walls of Pueblo Bonito (below) in Chaco Canyon.

Even before these ancient people were cultivating crops, though, they left rock art traces of themselves. Etched in the desert varnish at the Sand Island Petroglyph Site, just west of Bluff, Utah, for example, are hundreds of images spanning many eras, ranging from early spirals and other abstract symbols to broad-shouldered humans with enigmatic crescents above their heads, and later representations of animals and the Anasazi flute player called Kokopelli. Farther north, around Moab, are scores of equally vivid panels, including some that show "paper doll cutouts"; bears, snakes, and elk; and, much later, men on horseback.

Though we can only guess at the exact meaning of these figures, they give tantalizing clues to the artists' worldviews. Hints about the artists' day-to-day lives can be found in the remains of nearby villages, which vary in size from gigantic structures that could house thousands to tiny dwellings that probably held only a family or two. These sites represent several different cultures that thrived here between 8th and 12th centuries C.E.

The Hohokam were centered roughly near Phoenix, though their settlements extended as far north as Flagstaff. Farmers known for their irrigation systems, they traded widely and played ball games that resembled those of Mesoamerica.

The Mogollon, who ranged from the mountains of central Arizona into New Mexico, constructed pueblos with underground chambers, and around 900 C.E. created the unmistakable black-and-white Mimbres pots that are museum treasures today.

The Anasazi lived in the Four Corners area and are responsible for many other sites in addition to Mesa Verde, including the monumental Chaco Canyon community. Perhaps 5,000 people lived here, in nine structures that included the crescent-shaped Pueblo Bonito, as well as trading and ceremonial centers. There was also a huge network of roads that radiated across the desert toward outlying settlements. West of Mesa Verde, at Hovenweep National Monument, the Anasazi erected striking round, square, and D-shaped towers on the rim of a narrow canyon. At

Ruins of a Franciscan mission from 1621 are preserved at Jemez State Monument (above). *San Lorenzo de Picuris Mission Church* (top right) *remains a vital part of Picuris Pueblo.* Top: *Some sites at Bandelier National Monument require a climb.*

Canyon de Chelly, Arizona, they carved out beautiful cliff dwellings overlooking a serene canyon floor.

South of Flagstaff, the Sinagua people, perhaps influenced by the Anasazi, built a small pueblo at Tuzigoot and a cliff dwelling now called Montezuma's Castle, due to the cultural arrogance of a 19th-century writer who assumed that the impressive architecture had to be the work of Aztecs.

All this construction called for great organization and effort. Yet, by the end of the 1200s, virtually all the sites were abandoned. Some Anasazi evidently pushed into the Rio Grande Valley, where they lived in the pueblo-like rooms of Bandelier National Monument, though within 200 years they were gone from there, too.

Despite the mystery of why, exactly, these groups left their homes, archaeologists now believe that they never completely disappeared from the Southwest. The descendants of the Hohokam can be linked to today's Ood'ham peoples, while the Hopi and the 19 modern pueblo tribes – from Acoma to Zuni – are believed to be inheritors of the Mogollon and Anasazi cultures.

Acoma Pueblo's "Sky City" sits atop a 367-foot-high butte that rises from a dry, flat valley in western New Mexico. The pueblo has been inhabited since around 1150 C.E., making it, along with the Hopi village of Oraibi and Taos Pueblo, one of the oldest continuously occupied communities in the United States.

Today the Acoma tribal council maintains a gorgeous new cultural center as well as a busy casino, but its spiritual heart is on the mesa top, where a dozen families live in traditional adobe dwellings, without running water or electricity. (Other tribal members have houses on the

valley floor and return for ceremonial occasions.) Central to the village is the church of San Esteban del Rey, completed in 1641, and graced by a vividly painted *retablo* blending sun, moon, and stars with an image of the patron saint.

Of all the pueblos, Taos may be the most familiar, thanks to the paintings of the Taos School artists. It, too, has been home to Native Americans for roughly a millennium, and its arrangement of adobe dwellings around a dusty plaza seems utterly unchanged throughout the centuries. It was here, in 1680, that the Pueblo Revolt began, successfully driving the Spanish from this part of New Spain for two decades. Though they also maintain ceremonial kivas, contemporary villagers worship in San Geronimo Church, built in 1706. At the edge of the cemetery is the ruined bell tower of the original mission, a sad reminder of retaliation meted out on the community after the death of Governor William Bent in Taos town during the Mexican–American War.

Unlike the Pueblo tribes, the Navajos and the Apaches – related by language – migrated into the Southwest sometime between 1000 and 1500 C.E., filling in the territories left emptying territories as earlier peoples moved on. Navajos eventually became sheepherders and weavers, while the Apache bands historically relied on trading and raiding. To the north, the Utes represented still another tradition, moving into the Great Basin around 1250 C.E. and from there to the Rocky Mountains. They were able to maintain their nomadic way of life until the late 1800s, when overwhelming waves of settlers pushed them into ever-smaller parcels of land.

By the turn of the century, Native American territories had been sliced into reservations, and the railroad and the ranchers were changing a

At Acoma Sky City (top left and right), *a ladder leads to a rooftop entrance of a kiva, and a potter shows off her finely decorated wares. Indian pottery, rugs, jewelry, and other crafts have been offered since 1916 at Cameron Trading Post, which also uses examples in its hotel rooms* (above).

The annual Navajo Nation Fair in Window Rock, Arizona, features rodeo events (left), *arts and crafts, Indian food, song and dance, and, sometimes, a handsome cowgirl* (above).

landscape that was already drawing sightseers. Trading posts sprang up near Navajo and Hopi lands, supplying goods to the Indians in exchange for wool, blankets, and animals, and in the process helping to introduce their crafts to a wider market.

Hubbell's Trading Post in Ganado, Cameron Trading Post near the Grand Canyon, and Goulding's in Monument Valley have continued in business, adding lodges and restaurants to the goods – often museum quality – for sale in their historic buildings. Navajo weaving and jewelry, Hopi and Pueblo pottery, Zuni turquoise jewelry, Ute beadwork, Apache baskets, and much more are on display, along with memorabilia from the trading posts' early days.

Exquisite and rare crafts, along with the paintings and sculptures of contemporary Native American artists, also fill the galleries of Southwestern museums, from the once-private collections of the Millicent Rogers Museum in Taos to the modern Edge of the Cedars State Park Museum in Blanding, Utah, and the new Haak'u Museum at Acoma's Sky City Cultural Center.

Of course, objects, however beautiful, represent only part of a culture. Native Americans have also kept their traditions alive through ritual observances, dances, storytelling, and pow-wows. Many of these events are open to outsiders, introducing visitors to a living heritage that is fundamental to understanding the Southwest.

Utah

Bluff

THE OLD HILLTOP pioneer cemetery in Bluff is a scenic and peaceful spot. From here it's easy to make out Cottonwood Wash, which descends from the Abajo Mountains in the north. Closer at hand are the massive stone buttes that suggested the town's original name – Bluff City. Each rock now has its own evocative title: Locomotive Rock vaguely resembles a train, while the towers on either side are the Twin Rocks, after the Navajo Twins of that tribe's creation myths.

In the cemetery itself, smooth cobbles mark off the graves whose markers recall the life journeys of Bluff's founding families. One headstone reads "Jens Nielson, Born 1820, Died 1886. Crossed the Plains in the Hand Cart Company." Another commemorates a settler's birth in Ireland in 1822 and death in Bluff 80 years later, while a third, for a ten-month-old baby, is a testament to the difficulty of survival in those times.

Founded officially on April 6, 1880, Bluff was the final destination of the Mormon party responsible for the Hole-in-the-Rock Trail through what is now Grand Staircase-Escalante National Monument. Blasting a wagon route down a narrow crevice above the Colorado River, they crossed the river on rafts, and continued to this spot among the cottonwoods on the San Juan River.

The Mormon settlers intended to set up a farming community. The first step was to build a large square fort enclosing a series of one-room, sod-roofed log cabins, along with a meetinghouse, trading post, and blacksmith shop. Most of the fort has disappeared, except for the home of Joseph and Harriet Barton, who connected three cabins into a house large enough for themselves and their seven children. That structure – the oldest in the town – has been preserved with its rough plank floors and log walls, while the meeting-

*E*ons of geophysical forces have sculpted the cliffs and canyons along the breathtaking road between Boulder and Escalante. (Page 165)

*D*oubly impressive, the sandstone pillars known as Twin Rocks (opposite) *are easily recognizable landmarks in Bluff, which was established in 1880 by Mormon pioneers. For a few years, the settlers lived in rough cabins grouped to form a square fort. Though most of the original buildings have deteriorated, the log-walled structure that served as a chapel and courtroom (below) was recently reconstructed.*

A bend in the San Juan River produces the Goosenecks (opposite), exposing rocks 300 million years old. The "castle" at Hovenweep National Monument (above) was abandoned by its inhabitants 700 years ago. Left: A handsome 19th-century brick home in the Bluff historic district.

house – once the scene of worship, court proceedings, and social dances – was recently reconstructed.

By 1883 most newcomers had moved to larger town lots and planted crops, but a flood a year later drove many settlers away. The remaining families turned to raising cattle and built the substantial homes that make up Bluff's historic district. Victorian in style, but mostly made of native sandstone bricks, the dwellings reflect the prosperity of the turn of the century, before the erratic flow of the San Juan River and the difficulties of irrigating led to the town's decline.

In recent years, however, the river has attracted people back to Bluff, particularly travelers fascinated by the history – manmade and natural – of this corner of the Southwest. Guides lead raft expeditions through canyons accessible no other way, allowing visitors to marvel at fossilized sea creatures, petroglyphs, geological wonders, and elusive wildlife such as bighorn sheep.

Three rooms, spectacular view – the small cliff dwelling known as River House (above) *affords hikers a sense of apartment living,* c. *900* C.E.

Hundreds of petroglyphs are on view at Sand Island, a popular put-in spot for rafters. Other sites on the San Juan River, like Butler Wash further downstream, reveal evidence of thousands of years of human habitation. Some of the most noted petroglyphs at that site show enormous anthropomorphic figures – shamans perhaps – with enigmatic bars over their heads, as well as animals and abstract spiral signs.

At another stop, a short hike leads to River House, a three-room cliff dwelling built around 900 C.E. Snake pictographs decorate the ceiling of rooms that still have their T-shaped doorways and bricked-up storage areas. The Four Corners area abounds with cliff dwellings, many much larger than this. Hovenweek, for example, with its towers and "castle," lies just 30 miles east of Bluff. But River House seems especially intimate, rewarding those who make the river journey with a personal glimpse back in time.

*M*arcus Buck of Wild River Expeditions steers a raft down the San Juan (left) on a day trip that combines adventure with education. The riverbanks (above) offer a larger-than-life lesson in geology and history, with side excursions to see petroglyphs, dinosaur tracks, and abandoned mine works. Bighorn sheep sometimes make a shore-side appearance (opposite).

Escalante & Boulder

For about 20 miles, between tiny Escalante and tinier Boulder, Utah's exhilarating Route 12 twists its way past undulating slickrock, across the wild Escalante River, through rugged red canyons, and over a frighteningly narrow precipitous ridge called The Hogback. Constructed in 1940 and only com-pletely paved in 1971, the scenic byway has brought visitors to these two once-remote villages, whose homes and ranches evoke recall their beginnings a century ago.

Despite the difficult location, it's not hard to find evidence of human settlement here that goes much further back. In a canyon on the edge of Escalante, a panel of pictographs attributed to the Anasazi – a group of ancestral puebloan farmers who thrived from 1 to about 1400 C.E. – show a bighorn sheep, an atlatl-thrower, a figure of a bird-human, and the flute player known as Kokopelli, among other images. Outside Boulder, the Anasazi State Park Museum preserves the ruins of a village from the mid-12th century. Low stone walls clearly define the square dwellings and storerooms of the substantial settlement, which was surrounded by fields of corn, beans, and squash but inexplicably abandoned after 75 years.

Officially designated a Scenic Byway, Route 12 (above) lives up to its name with slickrock panoramas and canyon curves between Escalante and Boulder. Completed in 1940, the road finally opened up automobile access to communities that previously got mail on muleback. Right: A "family circle" is part of a vivid panel of pictographs near Escalante.

Underneath the modern siding of a café (below) *lies a log cabin from 1880, possibly the second that went up in Escalante. The town's wide streets reflect Mormon urban planning, which traditionally divided 5-acre squares into four lots with room for a house, barn, granary, and other outbuildings on each section.*
Right: *Like a three-dimensional Rorschach test, a rock outcrop in Escalante-Grand Staircase National Monument tempts onlookers to find some familiar shape.*

Mormon pioneers explored the Escalante region in 1875 and founded a town the following year, dividing the land into 5-acre plots and doling out a spacious quarter-section to each family. They chose the name to honor Fray Silvestre Vélez de Escalante, a Spanish missionary who had tried to find a route through Utah to California a century earlier. Many of the settlers' houses have survived, along with outlying barns and granaries.

The earliest log cabins in Escalante quickly evolved to federal-style colonials and gabled Queen Anne dwellings, often constructed of locally made brick, with thick walls, high ceilings, and fireplaces – all elements prized by the artists and preservationists who have begun to buy and restore the town's dwellings. A similar trove of turn-of-the-century red-brick houses awaits architecture aficionados in the historic district of Panguitch, about 60 miles to the west.

Boulder, however, is more a collection of ranches around a central crossroads than a planned settlement. Established in 1889 on the east side of the hard-to-bridge Escalante River, it now boasts several guest lodges that cater to outdoors adventurers who hike,

bike, or jeep the daunting high-country trails, which have names like Hell's Backbone, and once were the only means of access to the town.

In fact, it is the challenging – and spectacular – terrain that attracts most travelers to the sights along Utah's Scenic Route 12. In Bryce Canyon National Park, ancient sediments have been eroded over the millennia to fantastic spires of pinkish rock called hoodoos, while larger panoramas that suggest castles, gardens, or thrones of the gods.

A few miles south of Route 12, the showy spires and hoodoos of Bryce Canyon's Inspiration Point (opposite) emerge from a late-season blanket of snow. Further east, Escalante's Main Street (above) brightens its low profile with a few eye-catching façades. The People's Exchange (left) has a brick false-front; it began as a co-op around 1901.

At Kodachrome Canyon State Park, the action of wind and water on rock has left dramatic cones, towers, and pyramids that are the relics of volcanic sand pipes; in Escalante Petrified Forest State Park a hike around the mesa-top brings one to the vividly fossilized chunks of wood that began as trees submerged in mud perhaps 150 million years ago.

Grand Staircase-Escalante National Monument protects its own vast wilderness of cliffs, plateaus, wild canyons, and striking rock formations. In the area called Devil's Garden, for example, sandstone has been shaped by the elements to resemble Egypt's Colossi of Memnon or Easter Island's gargantuan heads.

Only a few unpaved roads cross the monument. The 57-mile Hole-in-the-Rock Road follows the path forged by Mormon pioneers to a cliff above the Colorado River, where they blasted a trail out of a crevice and lowered their wagons to the water.

This rugged and difficult terrain is truly a landscape that inspires. Perhaps this is why the artists of Escalante welcome visitors to an arts festival every autumn that includes a popular competition for painting in plein air.

A stroll along the paths that criss-cross Devil's Garden (right) can be a heady experience. Below: On a mesa-top in Escalante Petrified Forest State Park, the organic matter in ancient logs has been mineralized, producing rainbow-colored bands in the rocks.

Kanab

The immense crimson butte rises behind Kanab like a steamship moored at an invisible town pier. But the rock formation actually provides a clue to the town's place in its surrounding landscape, the colorful geological levels called the Grand Staircase of the Colorado Plateau. The oldest, bottom Chocolate Layer forms the north rim of the Grand Canyon. Next come Kanab's own Vermilion Cliffs, laid down as silt and dunes between 165 and 200 million years ago. The White Cliffs enclose Zion National Park, topped by the Gray Layer, and finally by the Pink

Cliffs – just 50 to 60 million years old – which contain Bryce Canyon National Park's stone spires and hoodoos.

Though Kanab has become a popular base for excursions to these nearby national parks, fewer people are familiar with the wilderness on its doorstep. Grand Staircase-Escalante National Monument was created by President Clinton in 1996 in a move denounced by locals, who preferred to keep the area open for business and mining. But, like the constantly shifting, wind-sculpted hills in neighboring Coral Pink Sand Dunes

State Park, attitudes have altered with the times. The striking mesas and eerie slot canyons of the 1.9-million-acre monument are now a valued part of Kanab's recreational offerings.

The town began with a fort built in 1869 but was abandoned to Indian attacks soon afterward. In 1870 Mormon ranchers returned and named the place Kanab – from the Ute word for "willows" – plotting out a generous grid that accounts for the wide streets and large house lots. A number of their turn-of-the century residences and businesses remain, from eclectic brick

Victorian homes to the 1892 general store that is now Main Street's popular Rocking V Café.

Best known is the gracious Heritage House, with its bottle-green columns and imposing square tower. Built in 1894, it later became the home of Thomas Chamberlain, a prominent citizen who lived there with one of his 6 wives and some of his 55 children. Since 1974, the house has been maintained as a museum with a wood-burning stove in the kitchen, an organ in the parlor, and clothes in the wooden armoire in the downstairs bedroom. Also among the exhibits are photos of Mary

A civic "K" for Kanab decorates a massive butte behind town (above left), while the Vermilion Cliffs beckon at the end of Center Street (above). This local scenery merely whets the appetite for the panoramic wonders that extend across 1.9 million acres in Grand Staircase-Escalante National Monument (top).

Kanab • 179

Hikers find a path on the unearthly slopes of Coral Pink Sand Dunes State Park (above), *the result of high winds wearing down sandstone landforms and funneling the grains through a mountain notch. Iron oxides account for the rosy hue.*

Chamberlain, Thomas's fifth wife, who was elected Kanab's mayor in 1912 – after being nominated as a prank – with an all-woman city council, almost a decade before national women's suffrage.

Another colorful member of the family, Garth Chamberlain had a football career and small movie roles before he transformed a sandstone grotto into a dancehall and drinking establishment in 1952. A rock hound and accomplished sculptor, Chamberlain

amassed collections that are on display in the quirky Moqui Cave museum continued by his son.

Other Kanab residents found part-time work in films as early as 1924, when cowboy star Tom Mix filmed *Deadwood Coach* in the area, with the help of the enterprising Parry brothers, who transported cast and crew from location to location. The Parrys lobbied other companies to film around Kanab, and built a colonial-style lodge to house the moviemakers. Today,

The elegant 1894 Heritage House (above) showcases Kanab's history. Movie ties linger in the Parry Lodge's theatrical barn (left) and the Gunsmoke gallows (below).

photos in the hotel remember guests like Glenn Ford and Claire Trevor, who starred in *The Desperadoes*; Frank Sinatra, Dean Martin, and Peter Lawford in *Sergeants 3*; and Clint Eastwood in *The Outlaw Josey Wales*, among many, many others.

All around Kanab, the roads lead to landscapes made familiar in countless movies and TV, like the ominous rock swirls called Ambush Point, or the outcrop where Clayton Moore – the Lone Ranger himself – called out

"Hi-Yo, Silver!" Beneath the sandstone cliffs of Johnson Canyon, however, the remains of the set for *Gunsmoke* look like they might teeter into oblivion.

Back in Kanab, Frontier Movie Town does its part to continue the tradition with a display of movie façades, which it uses for cookouts, Western shows, and the occasional tourist or student filmmaker who can't resist shooting a video about a gunfight, a gold mine, or a good guy with a horse who always gets the girl.

Manti, Spring City & Ephraim

LIKE A GREAT stone palace with two tall towers, the enormous Manti Utah Temple crowns a knoll in the Sanpete Valley, a gleaming white landmark visible for miles around. Built of local limestone and completed in 1888, the Temple is a striking backdrop for the Mormon Miracle Pageant, which chronicles the saga of Mormon prophet Joseph Smith and his followers' journey to Utah in 1847.

The annual cast-of-hundreds production reflects the Latter Day Saints' role in the history of the valley. In 1849, Brigham Young sent a party of settlers to these fertile lands below the Wasatch Plateau. Overtaken by winter snow, the party carved dugout shelters in the side of a hill and waited until spring, when they could construct cabins and a rough fort that would protect them from Indians.

Other communities soon dotted the valley. Twenty miles north, James Allred laid out the beginnings of Spring City in 1852, but Native American raids forced its residents to retreat to Manti. Two years later the group helped build another fort in Ephraim, closer to Spring City. But it would be 1859 before the settlers from Spring City returned home.

Today the three towns – Manti, Spring City, and Ephraim – are showcases for 19th-century architecture and Mormon town planning. Scores of surviving houses – solidly constructed of limestone quarried from the surrounding hills – are interspersed with more fanciful brick Victorians. Many of the earliest settlers were Scandinavian converts, whose carpentry skills account for the detailed woodworking.

Despite their linked history, each town developed its own personality. In the county seat of Manti, the John Patten House, built in 1854, is now a museum that illustrates what domestic life was like for the family of a farmer and agricultural engineer, from the period furniture in the downstairs sitting room to the clothes in the second-story bedrooms, where his 13 children slept.

Among Manti's other century-old structures are the residences of the stonemasons who built the Temple,

A gleaming limestone beacon to Mormon believers, the Manti Utah Temple (opposite above) has stood atop its hill since 1888. Architect William Folsom designed the four-story building with two monumental towers (opposite right). Though only the faithful may enter, anyone can attend the annual pageant (opposite left) on its grounds. The town itself was established in 1849, and dozens of pioneer structures survive in the neighborhoods bordering Main Street (left).

The Kenneth Bench home (above), from 1860, features the local limestone popular in Manti. A schoolroom (right) on the grounds of the 1854 John Patten House is part of a museum. Ephraim landmarks include (opposite, clockwise from top) Snow College, the historic Co-op, and an 1895 cottage-turned-inn.

the stately Manti House Inn where church leaders often stayed, and the Italianate city hall from 1882, superbly renovated as a visitors' center.

Ephraim has been home to Snow College since 1888, and the students of the two-year school add their own flavor to the Main Street historic district. A pizza parlor, for example, occupies the ground floor of the turn-of-the-century Ephraim Hotel. A couple of blocks away, the 19th-century Co-op now houses a craft shop, and the community granary has become the Central Utah Art Center, a sophisticated gallery for contemporary exhibits. Across the street, Pioneer Park preserves three of the town's early cabins. It was here, under a now-spindly "peace tree," that Mormon and Indian elders signed a treaty in 1868. The agreement ended

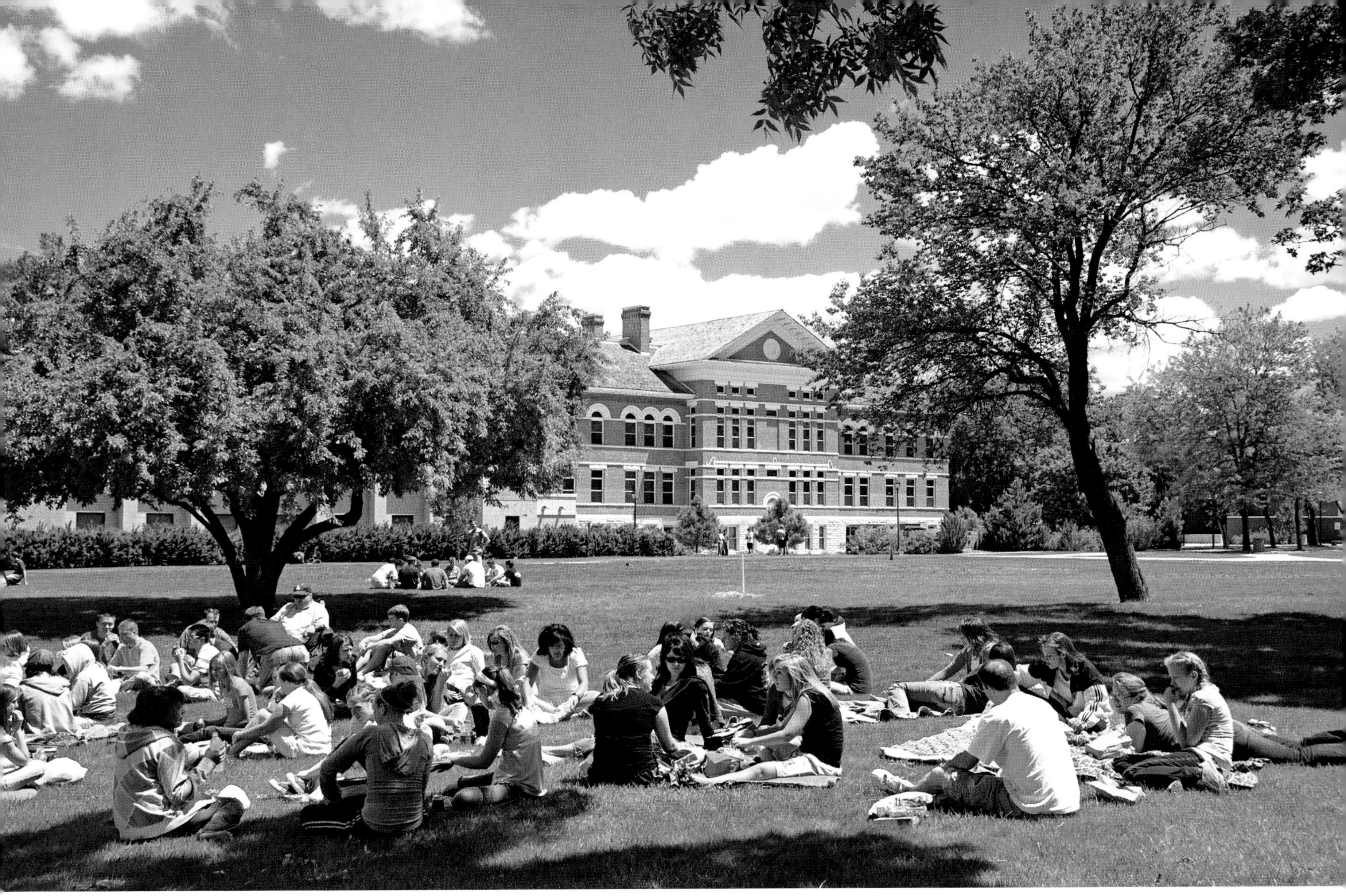

VACANCY
Pherson House
Bed & Breakfast

EPHRAIM CO-OP
Crafters & Artisans

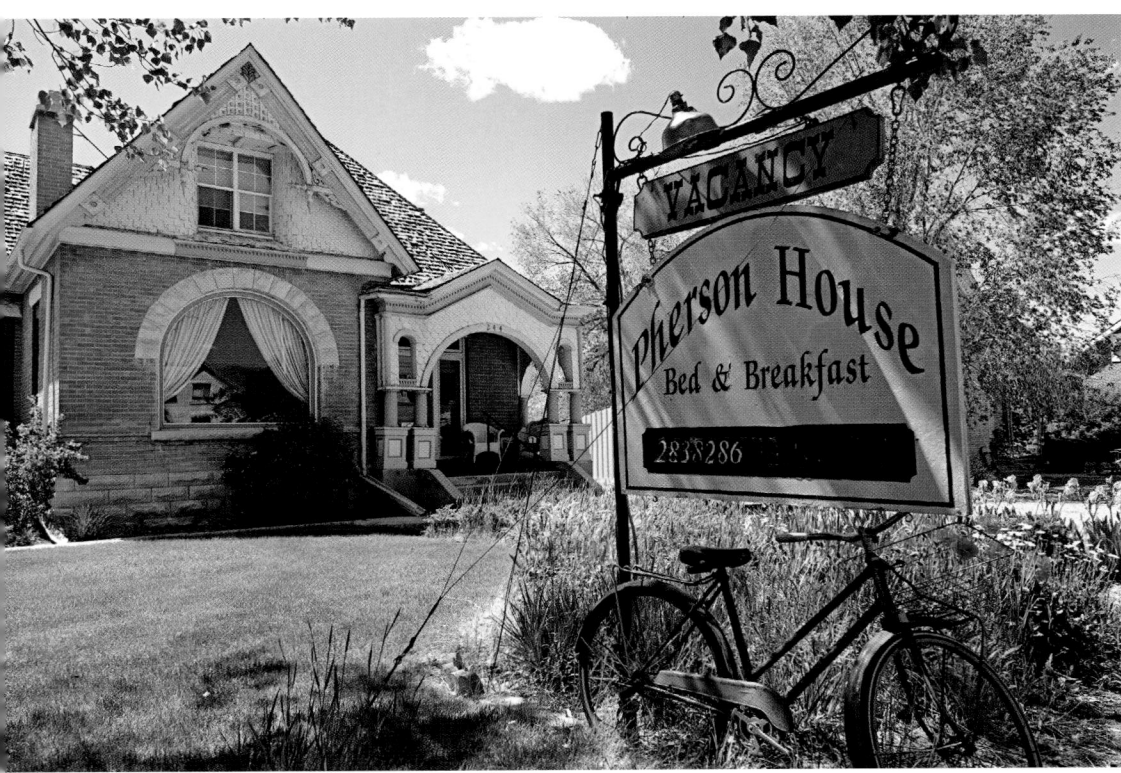

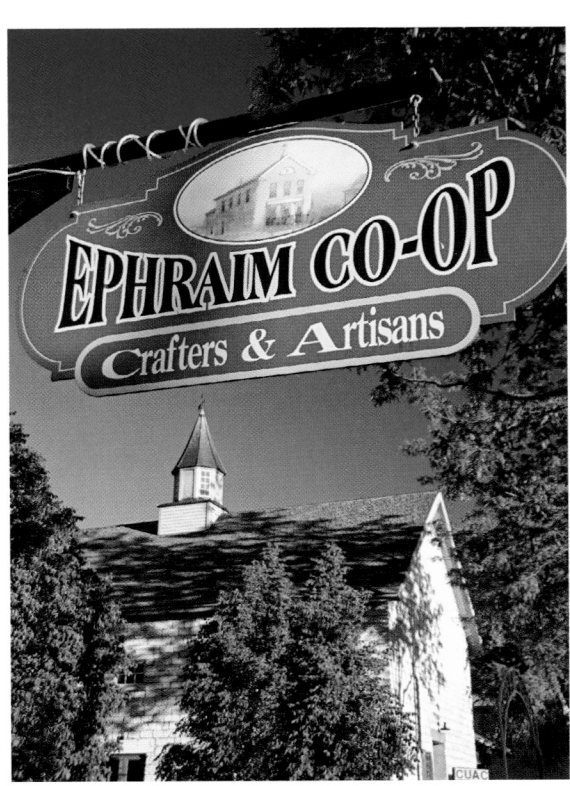

years of hostilities, promising to remain in force for as long as water flowed – as it still does through Pioneer Park – in Cottonwood Creek.

Over the decades this has remained an agricultural valley, dependent on sheep, then beets, and later turkeys. But times were often difficult. Spring City was almost a ghost town toward the end of the 20th century, with much of its 19th-century architecture crumbling and derelict. Yet in the 1970s a few artists were living in town, and gradually they were joined by others who bought and renovated its historic houses.

Among the targets of early preservation efforts was the limestone-brick Mormon chapel, built in 1902. Once a candidate for replacement, the chapel was defended by the local bishop, who successfully campaigned to save it. Today it's again a showpiece, resplendent with hand-carved woodwork, including gleaming pews, a curving suspended balcony, and ceiling beams that terminate in smiling cherubs.

On the next block is the imposing stone residence, built in 1868, that belonged to church apostle Orson Hyde. Across the street the elaborate Osborne House has been renovated as an inn. But Spring City's most spectacular home is a two-story Victorian mansion with a circular tower built by Jacob Johnson. The local judge

and U.S. congressman was said to have hobnobbed with every segment of Utah society, even sharing a cigar on the balcony with Butch Cassidy himself.

Spring City's "downtown" is essentially a crossroads with a gas station, a bed-and-breakfast-cum-antiques business, a tiny museum, and Victory Hall, which is being renovated as a theater. At the heart of the town is the lone café, a onetime confectionary from 1915, where you can enjoy breakfast or lunch along with the latest gossip and some good-natured teasing.

On the surrounding blocks are dozens of historic properties that house studios and galleries for the town's thriving art community, which includes painters, potters and ceramicists, a violinmaker, silversmiths, a chair maker, and a woodworker. There are frequent workshops and an annual studio tour, a plein-air painting competition, perhaps even an impromptu bluegrass festival. You bring your own chair. The music – and the community spirit of a bygone age – come free.

The snow-capped peaks of the Wasatch Plateau (right) *rise 5,000 feet above the Sanpete Valley, beckoning with recreational possibilities.* Below: *A bell tower tops artsy Spring City's former city hall, once a schoolhouse and now a museum. Behind the old firehouse's clapboard false front is another a historical collection.*

Moab

Just west of Moab, on the riverside cliff face known as Wall Street, agile rock climbers are working their way up regular bolted routes, spreadeagled on the vertical stone as they stretch to find a toe- or fingerhold. A few feet away, ancient petroglyphs celebrate the achievements of the peoples who lived here perhaps a millennium ago. Images of paper-doll figures holding hands, mysterious shamans with elaborate headdresses, and bighorn sheep being chased into corrals offer tantalizing glimpses of several vanished cultures.

Here on these rocks Moab's enigmatic past encounters Moab's adventurous future. In a region where ancient Native Americans traded, hunted, and practiced their spiritual beliefs, outdoor enthusiasts are finding new ways to revel in the spectacular natural landscape.

The town is surrounded by awe-inspiring scenery. Beginning almost at the town's northern boundary, Arches National Park is dotted by scores of red-gold sandstone formations, including balanced rocks and

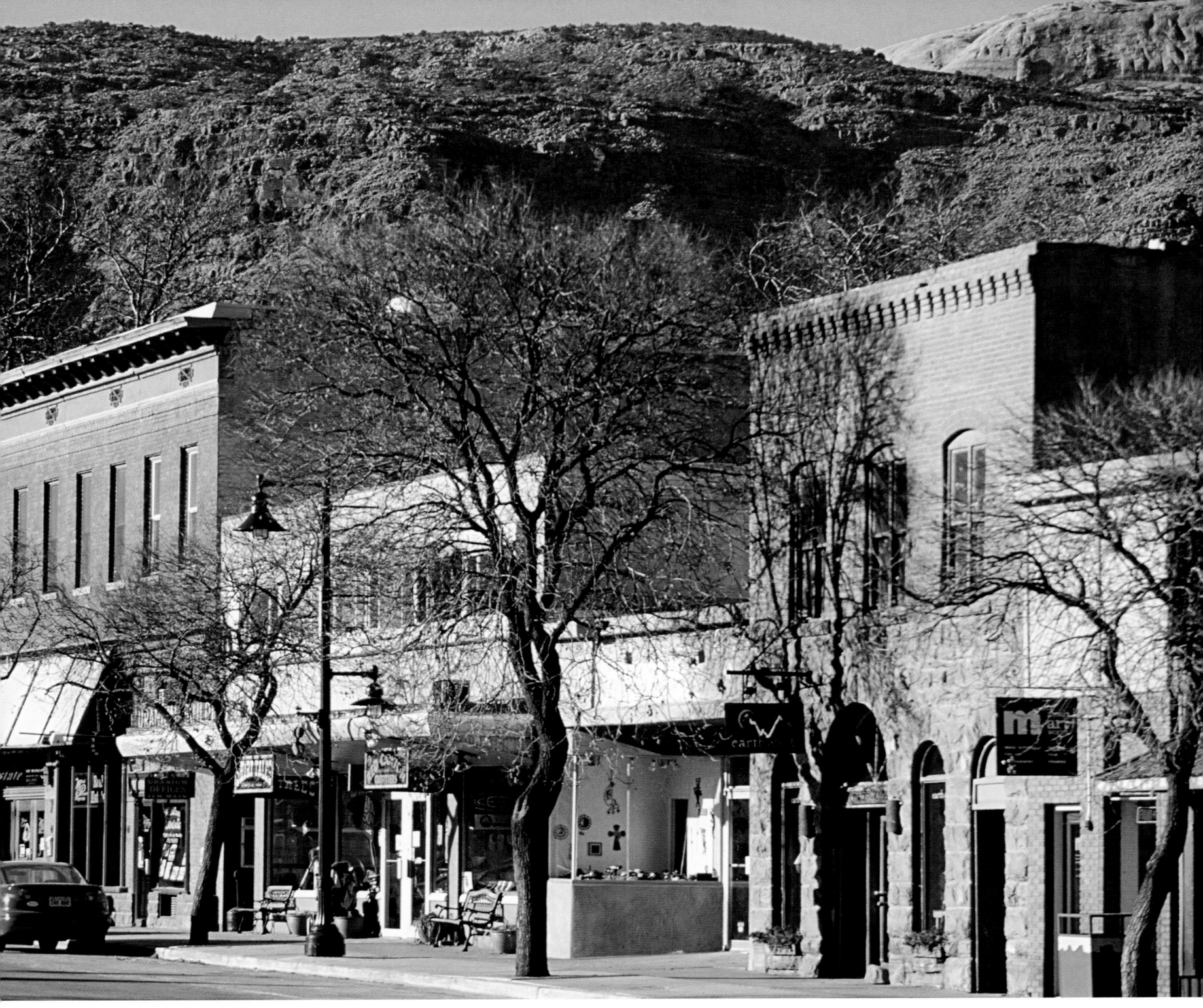

fortress-like outcrops. The "fins" that have been created by the action of wind and water on the shifting layers of an underground salt bed have crumbled into the park's signature rock arches, some astonishingly delicate, that soar into the Utah sky.

A few miles away, the Island in the Sky section of Canyonlands National Park, isolated by the confluence of the Colorado and Green Rivers, protects a vast wilderness of buttes, eroded ledges, and magnificent tiered sandstone benches.

Franciscan padres Dominguez and Escalante pioneered the Old Spanish Trail through this impenetrable terrain in 1776, blazing a path through Moab that was used by traders and fur trappers until the mid-1800s. In 1855 Mormon missionaries tried to found a town here but were driven off almost immediately by the fierce Ute Indians. Twenty years would pass before ranchers and farmers finally settled in the area.

A handful of structures go back to the community's early days. There's an early log cabin from 1881; the

Moab's turn-of-the-century stretch of Main Street (above) *caters to creature comforts. The wonders of Arches National Park, including Courthouse Towers* (opposite above) *and Double Arch* (oppostie below)*, offer more elemental pleasures.*

Cattlemen-merchants ran their business from the Cooper-Martin Building (right), finished in 1907. The two-celled jail (above) doubled as a courthouse long before it was a café.

first Latter Day Saints Church, built in 1888; and a few brick mercantile buildings from the late 1890s on Main Street that today house shops or restaurants. Even the small courthouse and two-cell jail has become a popular café.

Local cattlemen and merchants built residences that reflected their late-19th-century success. A few graceful examples of Victorian or farmhouse-style homes are left, notably the grand Taylor house, built in 1896, and now the Desert Bistro Restaurant.

In its early days Moab was known for cattle ranching and its peach and pear orchards, though uranium discovered in the area in the 1890s was a harbinger of things to come. The ranches would also play a role in the movie industry, which produced epics like John Ford's *Rio Grande*, starring John Wayne, on the scenic rangeland. Filming continued here long after Westerns had faded in popularity. The heroines of *Thelma and Louise* famously ended their road trip by driving their automobile off Moab's Dead Horse Point, and one of the mannequins used in the filming of that stunt is enshrined in the Movie Museum on Red Cliffs Ranch.

In the early 1950s a maverick geologist named Charles Steen discovered commercial uranium deposits outside Moab, ushering in an economic boom that lasted for three decades. Steen himself made and lost a fortune, and by the 1980s the market for uranium had collapsed.

Not for four-wheel amateurs, the tortuously exhilarating Shafer Trail Road (right) *hairpins its way from an overlook in Canyonlands National Park down to the Colorado River. Acrophobes might prefer a white-water raft trip* (bottom) *through the park's thrilling rapids. Experienced cyclists are lured by the challenge of the 10.5-mile Slickrock Trail* (below).

After the uranium bust, another kind of riches began to draw people to Moab. The work of iconoclastic writer Edward Abbey – who had once been a seasonal ranger at Arches – focused attention on the beauty of the surroundings, and before long outdoor adventurers, especially bikers who sought out the steeply exhilarating Slickrock Trail, had discovered the town.

Today mountain bikers and skinny-tire enthusiasts come to test themselves, as do those who ride jeeps and Hummers up vertical slopes in search of spectacular vistas and extreme thrills. River rafters can choose between easy, flat stretches and intense rapids, such as those in Cataract Canyon. Hikers can follow trails to glorious canyons, awesome overlooks, and campsites far from all vestiges of modern life, while the rocks beckon climbers to ever greater heights.

Park City

The belfry of stately Washington School, constructed in 1889 and now an inn, rises over restored homes on Park Avenue (opposite). Thanks to ordinances governing historic structures, town façades are preserved, though interiors may be modernized and expanded. Park City's surrounding mountains rise to 10,000 feet, creating a world-class ski resort in winter and an appealing backdrop for summer biking on the Round Valley Loop (below).

THE SUMMER TEMPERATURE may be in the 80s and there's nary a flake of snow around Park City, but a crowd in shorts and tank tops has gathered at the Utah Olympic Park to watch several dozen skiers perfect their jumping technique. From athletes on the Chinese national team to local teenagers and grade-school day-campers, freestyle skiers wearing wetsuits and skis are propelling themselves down J-shaped ramps that deposit them, with varying degrees of skill and grace, into the bubbled surface of a swimming pool.

This park hosted the Nordic jumping, bobsled, luge, and skeleton events of the 2002 Winter Olympics, and its ski hills and tortuous bobsled track remain sites for competition and training, as well as speed-charged thrill rides open to the public. There's also the new Alf Engen Ski Museum, with interactive exhibits on the history of skiing in the region, and an entire floor devoted to Olympic memorabilia, from opening-ceremony costumes to Bode Miller's medal outfit.

The Olympics are a cherished chapter in the eventful story of Park City, whose early days were as bumpy as a slope of moguls. Centuries ago this part of the Wasatch Range was the territory of nomadic Ute Indians. After 1847, though, when Mormons led by Brigham Young moved to Salt Lake, some of the pioneers fanned out to the Wasatch canyons, too, carving out a toll road, establishing a sawmill, and setting up an overland stage stop.

However, it was mining, not Mormonism that gave birth to Park City. In the fall of 1868, soldiers stationed nearby were prospecting when they discovered promising ore on a ridge above 9,000 feet. They staked their "Flagstaff claim" with a bandanna and waited out the winter. When the metal turned out to be high-grade silver, a new rush to riches was on.

Though Brigham Young discouraged his followers from becoming miners, thousands of other fortune seekers poured in. Veterans of Nevada's Comstock Lode and immigrants from around the world came to work in

The caprices of the mountain climate can result in tulips with a topping of snow (above).

*R*eady for a stylish shopping spree, the picturesque façades of Main Street (above) arose after a devastating fire laid waste to downtown in 1898. Hilda, a women's clothing boutique, retains the sign of a long-ago incarnation (opposite above), while the statue of a moose outside Chloe (opposite below) changes garments with the owner's whim.

the 300 mines that eventually extracted lead, zinc, and copper, as well as silver. George Hearst, who had prospered in the Virginia City boom, bought the lucrative Ontario Mine in 1872, reaping some $50 million in profits. That same year the community was christened Parley's Park City, after Parley Parker Pratt, an early Mormon apostle, but the name was quickly abbreviated to Park City.

By 1889 the population had grown to 6,000 souls, and shops, banks, the *Park Record* newspaper office, and two dozen saloons clustered along Main Street. The

sturdy stone Washington School and the brick Congregational Church stood a block away on Park Avenue, while ladies of the evening entertained in 16 houses on the other side of town. Miners' cabins lined terraced streets on both sides of the canyon. With mills and smelters all around, and railroad tracks in the middle, Park City was a bustling, hardworking place.

Disaster struck in 1898, though, when a fire swept through the heart of Park City. Unfazed, the town's hardy residents rebuilt within 18 months.

Much of the charming historic district dates from the turn of the century, including brick boarding houses that accommodated miners; the First National Bank, whose vault is still inside an art gallery; and the telephone exchange that's now a stylish restaurant. The city hall, police station, jail, and fire station have been imaginatively renovated as the Park City Museum, which retells the town's story, from stagecoaches to ski lifts.

Despite the 1893 recession, the panic of 1907, ongoing labor troubles, and bad times during World War I, the mines sustained the economy, until the Depression and World War II proved too tough to overcome. The last mine – George Hearst's Ontario Mine – shut down in 1982, but by then the industry had already been moribund for decades. By the 1950s diehard old-timers would sit on their porches and watch as houses were loaded onto flatbed trucks and driven out of town. They couldn't see the new boom on the horizon.

Locals had long used skis to get around in winter. In the 1920s they had even begun ski jumping for fun

from a tailings pile outside the Creole Mine, as well as on nearby Ecker Hill. Government works projects built ski runs during the Depression, and a small-scale ski area sprang up near Deer Valley after World War II.

Then, in 1963, the United Park City Mines Company – which had consolidated ownership of most of the mountain land – opened Treasure Mountain, now Park City Mountain Resort. The company's mining background prompted a unique innovation: a "skiers' subway" carried sports enthusiasts down mining hoists and through the mountain on an old ore tram, before

depositing them out on the snowy slopes. Fortunately, chairlifts finally replaced the dark, damp journey.

The success of Treasure Mountain encouraged the building of more resorts – The Canyons in 1968, followed by Deer Valley in 1981. Since then Park City has become a chic destination, with restaurants, boutiques, art galleries, and hotels. The miners' cottages have been renovated into million-dollar properties, and the town has embraced reuse of historic structures with enthusiastic creativity, while architectural guidelines ensure that 19th-century façades are preserved. Even water

that once was a flood hazard in the mines is now channeled and purified for the local water supply.

In summer, families come to hike, bike, ride alpine coasters and ziplines, or simply play in the mountain setting. In winter, skiers and snowboarders revel on slopes known for their dry powder. And every January the town welcomes the Sundance Festival, Robert Redford's renowned showcase for independent films. For 12 days celebrities and movie buffs jam the historic Egyptian Theatre, built in 1926 with exotic decor, but outside, Park City itself has the starring role.

Bare aspens flank a pond in Wasatch Mountain State Park (above). *In town, footwear festoons the branches in so-called Shoe Tree Park* (opposite above). *At Utah Olympic Park* (below) *world-class skiers practice their jumps with a finish in the bubbly…water, that is.*

Places to Stay and Eat

ARIZONA

For more information: Arizona Office of Tourism, 866-275-5816; www.ArizonaGuide.com

Bisbee

For more information: Cochise County Tourism Council, 1415 Melody Lane, Building G, Bisbee, AZ 85603, 520-432-9215 or 800-862-5273 (toll-free within the USA), www.explorecochise.com. Bisbee Visitor Center, #2 Copper Queen Plaza and Convention Center, P.O. Box 1642, Bisbee, AZ 85603, 520-432-3554 or 866-224-7233 (toll-free within the USA), www.discoverbisbee.com.

Hotels

COPPER QUEEN COURTYARD HOTEL, 520-432-2216, www.copperqueen.com. Renovated century-old hotel, originally built by the Phelps Dodge Mining Company to lure visitors to Bisbee.

SHADY DELL, 520-432-3567, www.theshadydell.com. One-of-a-kind retro accommodation in vintage trailers.

Restaurants

BISBEE GRILLE, 520-432-6788. Steaks, pasta, and Southwestern dishes in a casual setting.

CAFÉ ROKA, 520-432-5153. Contemporary gourmet cuisine in a Main Street setting.

DOT'S DINER, 520-432-1112. 1950s-style diner for breakfast and lunch.

HIGH DESERT MARKET AND CAFÉ, 520-432-6775. Fresh organic salads and sandwiches and home-baked pastries.

WINCHESTER RESTAURANT, 520-432-2216. Steaks, chops, and seafood in the dining room of a historic hotel.

Jerome

For more information: Jerome Chamber of Commerce, P.O. Box K, Jerome, AZ 86331, 928-634-2900, www.jeromechamber.com.

Hotels

CONNOR HOTEL OF JEROME, 928-634-5006 or 800-523-3554 (toll-free within the USA), www.connorhotel.com. A historic hotel, built in 1898, with 12 beautifully renovated rooms, right on Main Street.

JEROME GRAND HOTEL, 928-634-8200 or 888-817-6788 (toll-free within the USA), www.jeromegrandhotel.com. A converted five-story Spanish Mission-style hospital, built in 1927, with restored rooms and a panoramic view over the valley.

Restaurants

BELGIAN JENNIE'S BORDELLO BISTRO & PIZZERIA, 928-639-3141. Italian specialties in a restaurant named for one of the town's famous shady ladies.

HAUNTED HAMBURGER, 928-634-0554. Burgers and sandwiches with a valley view.

GRAPES, 928-639-8477. A wine bar serving delicious pizzas and pastas.

MILE HIGH GRILL AND SPIRITS, 928-634-3330. Hearty breakfasts and lunches in a renovated 1899 building.

Prescott

For more information: Prescott Chamber of Commerce, 117 W. Goodwin Street, Prescott, AZ 86302, 928-445-2000, www.visit-prescott.com.

Hotels

HASSAYAMPA INN, 928-778-9434 or 800-322-1927 (toll-free within the USA), www.hassayampainn.com. Beautifully restored historic 1927 hotel, with an elegant Art Deco dining room.

HOTEL VENDOME, 928-776-0900 or 888-468-3583 (toll-free within the USA), www.vendomehotel.com. Charmingly renovated 1917 bed-and-breakfast inn one block from the courthouse.

LOG CABIN BED & BREAKFAST, 928-778-0442 or 888-778-0442 (toll-free within the USA), www.prescottlogcabin.com. Five charming rustic rooms in the Granite Dells.

PLEASANT STREET INN, 928-445-4774, 877-226-7128, www.pleasantbandb.com. Victorian bed-and-breakfast in a residential neighborhood.

PRESCOTT RESORT AND CONFERENCE CENTER, 928-776-1666 or 800-967-4637 (toll-free within the USA), www.prescottresort.com. Modern 160-room hotel and casino overlooking Prescott and run by the Yavapai Indian tribe.

Restaurants

CAFFE ST. MICHAEL, 928-776-1999. Stylish bistro in a turn-of-the-century hotel across from Courthouse Plaza.

DINNER BELL, 928-777-8853. Locals' favorite for a creek-side breakfast.

MONSOON, 928-776-0205. Pan-Asian dining near the Plaza.

MURPHY'S, 928-445-4044. Steaks and pub food in a renovated 1890s mercantile store.

THE PALACE RESTAURANT AND SALOON, 928-541-1996. Atmospheric bar and eatery in one of the most famous buildings on Whiskey Row.

THE ROSE RESTAURANT, 928-777-8308. Fine dining in a historic dwelling.

Sedona

For more information: Sedona Chamber of Commerce Tourism Bureau, P.O. Box 478, Sedona, AZ 86339, 928-282-7722 or 800-288-7336 (toll-free within the USA), www.VisitSedona.com.

Hotels

ENCHANTMENT RESORT AND MII AMO, a destination spa, 928-282-2900 or 800-826-4180 (toll-free within the USA), www.enchantmentresort.com. A deluxe resort and extensive spa nestled among the red rocks of Boynton Canyon.

THE INN ON OAK CREEK, 928-282-7896 or 800-499-7896 (toll-free within the USA), www.innonoakcreek.com. Upscale creekside bed-and-breakfast.

L'AUBERGE DE SEDONA, 928-282-1661 or 800-272-6777 (toll-free within the USA), www.lauberge.com. An elegant lodge and cottages on the banks of Oak Creek.

SKY RANCH LODGE, 928-282-6400 or 888-708-6400 (toll-free within the USA), www.skyranchlodge.com. Comfortable cottages and rooms with panoramic views.

Restaurants

BARKING FROG GRILLE, 928-804-2000. Mexican specialties in a hacienda setting.

COWBOY CLUB, 928-282-4200. Southwestern cuisine in a long-established uptown bar and restaurant.

DAHL & DILUCA, 928-282-5219. Locals' favorite spot for fine Italian dishes.

Tombstone

For more information: Cochise County Tourism Council, 1415 Melody Lane, Building G, Bisbee, AZ, 85603, 520-432-9215 or 800-862-5273 (toll-free within the USA), www.explorecochise.com. Tombstone Chamber of Commerce, P.O. Box 995, Tombstone, AZ 85638, 888-457-3929, www.cityoftombstone.com.

Hotels

BEST WESTERN LOOKOUT LODGE, 520-457-2223, or 800-652-6772 (toll-free within the USA), www.bestwesternarizona.com/tombstone-hotels. Modern motel at the edge of town, with nice views.

LARIAN HOTEL, 520-457-2272, www.tombstonemotels.com. Comfortable, well-kept motel in the historic district.

Restaurants

BIG NOSE KATE'S 1880 SALOON, 520-457-3405. Atmospheric bar and restaurant in the 1881 Grand Hotel building.

CRYSTAL PALACE SALOON, 520-457-3611. Bar and restaurant restored to its 1880 look.

LAMPLIGHT ROOM RESTAURANT, 520-457-3716. Mexican cuisine in a historic house, with music on weekends.

OK CAFÉ, 520-457-3980. Popular spot for home-cooked breakfasts and lunches.

Tumacácori & Tubac

For more information: Tubac Chamber of Commerce, 50 Bridge Road, B-8, P.O. Box 1866, Tubac, AZ 85646, 520-398-2704, www.tubacaz.com. Tubac Presidio State Historic Park, P.O. Box 1296, Tubac, AZ 85646, 520-398-2252, www.azstateparks.com. Tumacacori National Historical Park, P.O. Box 67, Tumacacori, AZ 85640, 520-398-2341, www.nps.gov/tuma.

Hotels

TUBAC COUNTRY INN, 520-398-3178, www.tubaccountryinn.com. Intimate bed-and-breakfast in a garden setting.

TUBAC GOLF RESORT & SPA, 520-398-2211, or 800-848-7893 (toll-free within the USA), www.tubacgolfresort.com. Upscale hacienda accommodation with a scenic golf course on a historic ranch.

Restaurants

THE ARTIST'S PALATE, 520-398-3333. Steak, seafood, pizza, and pasta in an artful setting.

THE STABLES RESTAURANT, 520-398-3178. Gourmet menu in an atmospheric renovated stable.

WISDOM'S CAFÉ, 520-398-2397. Long-established locals' favorite for Mexican cuisine.

COLORADO

For more information: Colorado Tourism Office, 800-COLORADO, www.colorado.com.

Aspen

For more information: Aspen Chamber Resort Association, 425 Rio Grande Place, Aspen, CO 81611, 970-925-1940 or 888-290-1324 (toll-free within the USA), www.aspenchamber.org.

Hotels

ASPEN MEADOWS RESORT, 970-925-4240 or 800-452-4240 (toll-free within the USA), www.dolce-aspen-hotel.com. Bauhaus-inspired all-suite resort on the grounds of the Aspen Institute.

HOTEL JEROME, 970-920-1000 or 800-331-7213 (toll-free within the USA), www.hoteljerome.com. Exquisitely renovated historic hotel, built by one of Aspen's founding fathers.

LIMELIGHT LODGE, 970-925-3025 or 800-433-0832 (toll-free within the USA), www.limelightlodge.com. Newly built property with mountain lodge decor.

MOUNTAIN CHALET, 970-925-7797 or 888-925-7797 (toll-free within the USA), www.mountainchaletaspen.com. Family-run ski lodge near Aspen Mountain.

SKY HOTEL, 970-925-6760 or 800-882-2582 (toll-free within the USA), www.theskyhotel.com. Upscale accommodation with a chic European vibe.

ST. REGIS RESORT, 970-920-3300 or 800-325-3589 (toll-free within the USA), www.stregis.com/aspen. Old World-style luxury hotel in downtown Aspen.

THE LITTLE NELL, 970-920-4600 or 888-843-6355 (toll-free within the USA), www.thelittlenell.com. Deluxe 92-room hostelry at the foot of Aspen Mountain.

Restaurants

CACHE CACHE, 970-925-3835. Classical French cooking meets American bistro.

MONTAGNA, 970-920-6330. Rocky Mountain cuisine in the dining room of The Little Nell.

OLIVE'S ASPEN, 970-920-7356. Mediterranean dishes at the elegant St. Regis Resort.

L'HOSTARIA, 970-925-9022. Sophisticated Italian cuisine.

MATSUHISA, 970-544-6628. Elegant Japanese dishes from innovative Chef Nobu.

PINONS, 970-920-2021. American cuisine in a stylish setting.

SIX89, 970-963-6890. Gourmet dining up-valley in Carbondale.

Breckenridge

For more information: Breckenridge Resort Chamber, P.O. Box 1909, 311 S. Ridge St., Breckenridge, CO 80424, 970-453-2913 or 877-234-3989 (toll-free within the USA), www.gobreck.com.

Hotels

BARN ON THE RIVER BED & BREAKFAST, 970-453-2975, or 800-795-2975 (toll-free within the USA), www.breckenridge-inn.com. Luxury bed-and-breakfast in a waterside setting.

GREAT DIVIDE LODGE, 970-547-5550 or 888-906-5698 (toll-free within the USA), www.breckresorts.com/greatdividelodge. Convenient comfortable condo accommodation.

LODGE & SPA AT BRECKENRIDGE, 970-453-9300 or 800-736-1607 (toll-free within the USA), www.thelodgeatbreck.com. Mountainside rooms with rustic chic decor.

MOUNTAIN THUNDER LODGE, 970-453-2000 or 800-800-7829 (toll-free within the USA), www.mountainthunderlodge.com. Spacious mountain-style rooms and suites five minutes from downtown Breckenridge.

Restaurants

COLUMBINE CAFÉ, 970-547-4474. Locals' favorite for breakfast.

GIAMPIETROS, 970-453-3838. Popular spot for pizza and classic pasta.

HEARTHSTONE, 970-453-7028. Fine dining in an elegant 1880s residence.

RELISH, 970-453-0989. New American cooking in a lively downtown setting.

THE CELLAR, 970-453-4777. Small plates and a tasting menu in a casually elegant 19th-century home.

Durango & Silverton

For more information: Durango Area Tourism Office, P.O. Box 2321, 111 S. Camino del Rio, Durango, CO 81302, 970-247-3500 or 800-525-8855 (toll-free within the USA), www.durango.org. Silverton Chamber of Commerce, P.O. Box 565, Silverton, CO 81433, 800-752-4494, www.silvertoncolorado.com.

Hotels

GENERAL PALMER HOTEL, 970-247-4747 or 800-523-3358 (toll-free within the USA), www.generalpalmerhotel.com. Luxury accommodation in a historic 1898 hotel near the Durango-Silverton Railroad Depot in Durango.

GRAND IMPERIAL VICTORIAN HOTEL, 970-387-5527 or 800-341-3340 (toll-free within the USA), www.grandimperialhotel.com. Atmospheric Victorian hotel on the main street in Silverton.

INN OF THE ROCKIES, 970-387-5336 or 800-267-5336 (toll-free within the USA), www.innoftherockies.com. Intimate inn in Silverton's 19th-century Alma House.

ROCHESTER HOTEL/THE LELAND HOUSE, 970-385-1920 or 800-664-1920 (toll-free within the USA), www.rochesterhotel.com.

Bed-and-breakfast rooms and suites in Durango's historic district.

STRATER HOTEL, 970-247-4431 or 800-247-74431 (toll-free within the USA), www.strater.com. Elaborate Victorian decor in a historic Durango hostelry from 1887.

TELLER HOTEL, 970-387-5423 or 800-342-4338 (toll-free within the USA), www.tellerhousehotel.com. Century-old nine-room hotel in the center of Silverton.

VILLA DALLAVALLE INN, 970-387-5555 or 866-387-5965 (toll-free within the USA), www.villadallavalle.com. Seven atmospheric rooms in a bed-and-breakfast in the center of Silverton.

Restaurants
CARVER BREWING COMPANY, 970-259-2545. Locally made beer, as well as a popular brunch spot in Durango.

CYPRUS CAFÉ, 970-385-6884. Mediterranean cuisine in a house and garden in Durango's historic district.

DIAMOND BELLE SALOON, 970-247-4431. Lively bar with Victorian decor in Durango's Strater Hotel.

GRUMPY'S SALOON AND RESTAURANT, 970-387-5527. 19th-century atmosphere, including a ragtime piano player, in Silverton's Grand Imperial Hotel.

HANDLEBARS, 970-387-5395. Antique and memorabilia-filled restaurant on Silverton's main street.

IRISH EMBASSY, 970-403-1200. Irish pub food and atmosphere on Durango's Main Street.

THE PICKLE BARREL RESTAURANT, 970-387-5713. Prime rib, seafood, burgers, and salads in a historic building in downtown Silverton.

Georgetown & Idaho Springs

For more information: Chamber and Tourism Bureau of Clear Creek County, Box 100, Idaho Springs, CO 80402, 303-567-4660 or 800-882-5278 (toll-free within the USA), www.clearcreekcounty.org; Historic Georgetown, Inc. 305 Argentine Street, P.O. Box 667, Georgetown, CO 80444, 303-569-2840, www.historicgeorgetown.org.

Hotels
HERITAGE INN, 303-567-4473, www.theheritageinn.com. Comfortable motel accommodation next to Clear Creek in Idaho Springs.

COLUMBINE INN, 303-567-0948, www.columbineinn.net. Sixteen rooms, suites, and cabins near Idaho Springs's historic district.

ALL ABOARD INN, 303-569-2525 or 888.992-2525 (toll-free within the USA), www.allaboardinn.com. Intimate bed-and-breakfast in a 19th-century Georgetown house.

ROSE STREET BED-AND-BREAKFAST, 303-569-2222 or 866-569-2221 (toll-free within the USA), www.rosestreetbedbreakfast.com. Three-room inn in Georgetown's historic district.

Restaurants
NEW PRAGUE RESTAURANT, 303-569-2861. Eastern European specialties in a cozy setting in Georgetown.

RED RAM RESTAURANT, 303-569-2300. Atmospheric saloon on Georgetown's main street.

THE BUFFALO, 303-567-2729. Buffalo dishes in a colorfully historic Idaho Springs restaurant.

TOMMYKNOCKERS BREWERY, 303-567-2688. Locally crafted beers and ales in a casual eatery.

TWO BROTHERS DELI, 303-567-2439. Longtime locals' spot for breakfast and lunch.

Ouray

For more information: Ouray Chamber Resort Association, P.O. Box 145, 1230 Main St., Ouray, CO 81427, 970-325-4746 or 800-228-1876 (toll-free within the USA), www.ouraycolorado.com.

Hotels
BEAUMONT HOTEL, 970-325-7000 or 888-447-3255 (toll-free within the USA), www.beaumonthotel.com. Exquisitely renovated 16-room historic property from 1887.

BOX CANYON LODGE, 970-325-4981 or 800-327-5080 (toll-free within the USA), www.boxcanyonouray.com. Comfortable motel accommodation with hot springs at the edge of downtown.

ST. ELMO HOTEL, 970-325-4951 or 866-243-1502 (toll-free within the USA), www.stelmohotel.com. Restored nine-room turn-of-the-century inn.

Restaurants
BACKSTREET BAGEL AND DELI, 970-325-0550. Gathering spot for breakfast and sandwiches.

THE BISTRO AT BILLY GOAT GRUFF'S, 970-325-4370. Sophisticated food in a casual Main Street setting.

THE OUTLAW, 970-325-4366. Longtime favorite for steak and prime rib.

THE TUNDRA RESTAURANT, 970-325-7070. Fine dining in a historic setting in the Beaumont Hotel.

THE WESTERN HOTEL RESTAURANT, 970-325-4645. Atmospheric saloon and Mediterranean dishes.

Steamboat Springs

For more information: Steamboat Springs Chamber Resort Association, P.O. Box 774408, 1255 South Lincoln Ave., Steamboat Springs, CO 80477, 970-879-0080, www.steamboat-chamber.com.

Hotels
HOTEL BRISTOL, 970-879-3083 or 800-851-0872 (toll-free within the USA), www.steamboathotelbristol.com. Intimate hotel in the town's historic district.

SHERATON STEAMBOAT HOTEL, 970-879-2220, www.sheraton.com/steamboat. Comfortable motel accommodation south of downtown.

STORM MEADOWS CLUB/MOUNTAIN RESORTS, 970-879-3700 or 888-262-5150 (toll-free within the USA), www.stormmeadows.com. Spacious condominium accommodation on Mt. Werner.

Restaurants
ANTARES, 970-879-9939. New American cuisine in a historic building

CAFÉ DIVA, 970-971-0508. Sophisticated dining with global flair in the ski base area.

CREEKSIDE CAFÉ, 970-879-4925. Breakfast and sandwich specialties in a waterside setting.

HARWIGS & L'APOGEE, 970-879-1919. Fine dining in a former saddlery on the main street.

MAHOGANY RIDGE BREWERY & GRILL, 970-879-3773. International "dipping entrees" and handcrafted beers.

ORE HOUSE AT THE PINE GROVE, 970-879-1190. Steaks and seafood served in a historic barn with Western ambience.

STEAMBOAT SMOKEHOUSE, 970-879-7427. Popular casual spot for ribs and barbecue.

Telluride

For more information: Telluride Tourism Board, P.O. Box 1009, 113 Lost Creek Lane, Suite A, Telluride, CO 81435, 888-605-2579 (toll-free within the USA), www.visittelluride.com.

Hotels
FAIRMONT HERITAGE PLACE FRANZ KLAMMER LODGE, 970-728-3318 or 888-728-3318 (toll-free within the USA), www.fairmont.com/klammerlodge. Luxurious suites in the heart of the Mountain Village.

HOTEL TELLURIDE, 970-369-1188 or 866-468-3501 (toll-free within the USA), www.thehoteltelluride.com. Lodge-style boutique hotel at the edge of downtown.

MOUNTAIN LODGE, 970-369-5000 or 866-368-6867 (toll-free within the USA), www.mountainlodgetelluride.com. Spacious accommodation with rustic chic decor in a ski-in, ski-out location.

NEW SHERIDAN HOTEL, 970-728-4351 or 800-200-1891 (toll-free within the USA), www.newsheridan.com. Newly renovated historic 1895 hotel on Telluride's main street.

RESORT QUEST, 970-728-6621 or 866-444-2108 (toll-free within the USA), www.resortquesttelluride.com. Real-estate company with a wide array of vacation rentals.

SAN SOPHIA INN, 970-728-3001 or 800-537-4781 (toll-free within the USA), www.sansophia.com. Upscale bed-and-breakfast hotel with a hint of Victorian style.

Restaurants

BAKED IN TELLURIDE, 970-728-4778. A local institution for pastries, breakfast, and sandwiches.

NEW SHERIDAN CHOP HOUSE RESTAURANT AND BAR, 970-728-9100. Bistro-style dining room and a historic saloon.

COSMOPOLITAN, 970-728-1292. Innovative contemporary cuisine.

EXCELSIOR CAFÉ, 970-728-4250. American cooking blending Rocky Mountain and classic Italian ingredients, served in an 1880s building.

FLORADORA SALOON, 970-728-8884. Burgers and sandwiches in a colorful, casual space.

HONGA'S LOTUS PETAL, 970-728-5124. Pan-Asian dishes in a historic building.

221 S. OAK, 970-728-9507. Eclectic menu served in an intimate 19th-century house.

Trinidad

For more information: Trinidad & Las Animas County Chamber of Commerce, 309 Nevada Avenue, Trinidad, CO 81082, 719-846-9512, www.historictrinidad.com.

Hotels

BEST WESTERN TRINIDAD, 719-846-2215 or 800-780-7234 (toll-free within the USA), www.bestwesterncolorado.com/trinidad-hotels. Comfortable motel close to the historic district.

TARABINO INN, 719-846-2115 or 866-846-8808 (toll-free within the USA), www.tarabinoinn.com. Bed-and-breakfast accommodation in a tastefully renovated Italianate mansion from the early 1900s.

Restaurants

BLACK JACK'S SALOON & STEAKHOUSE, 719-846-9501. Steaks, chicken, and ribs in a colorful Old West setting.

RINO'S ITALIAN RESTAURANT, 719-845-0949. Mediterranean cuisine in a 1890s house, complete with singing waiters.

THE CAFÉ, 719-846-7119. Sandwiches and pastries in a renovated Main Street building.

TRINIDAD BREWING COMPANY, 719-846-7069. Burgers, snacks, and handcrafted beers in the renovated Elm Street train station.

NEVADA

For more information: Nevada Commission on Tourism, 401 North Carson Street, Carson City, NV 89701, 775 687-4322 or 800-NEVADA-8 (toll-free within the USA), www.travelnevada.com.

Genoa

For more information: Carson Valley Chamber of Commerce and Visitors Center, 1477 U.S. Highway 395 N, Suite A, Gardnerville, NV 89410, 775-782-8144 or 800-727-7677

(toll-free within the USA), www.visitcarsonvalley.org.

Hotels

DAVID WALLEY'S RESORT, 775-782-8155 or 800-628-7831 (toll-free within the USA), www.davidwalleys.com. Modern suite accommodation on the site of a historic hot springs and spa.

GENOA HOUSE INN, 775-782-7075, www.genoahouseinn.com. Three-room bed-and-breakfast in an 1872 house.

THE WILD ROSE INN, 775-782-5697 or 877-819-4225 (toll-free within the USA), www.wildrose-inn.com. Spacious Victorian-style bed-and-breakfast inn in the center of Genoa.

Restaurants

DW's, 775-782-8155. Steak and seafood at David Walley's Resort.

GENOA COUNTRY STORE, 775-782-5694. Fresh sandwiches in a Main Street market.

JT'S BASQUE BAR & DINING ROOM, 775-782-2074. Family-style Basque meals in Gardnerville.

LA FERME, 775-783-1004. Fine French cuisine in a country setting in the heart of Genoa.

MARCELLO'S, 775-783-3211. Italian dishes in Minden.

Virginia City

For more information: Virginia City Convention & Tourism Authority, 86 S. C Street, P.O. Box 920, Virginia City, NV 89440, 775-847-7500 or 800-718-7587 (toll-free within the USA), www.visitvirginiacitynv.com.

Hotels

CHOLLAR MANSION, 775-847-9777 or 877-CHOLLAR (toll-free within the USA), www.chollarmansion.com. Three suites in the restored 1868 Chollar mine office and superintendent's home.

COBB MANSION BED & BREAKFAST, 877-847-9006, www.cobbmansion.com. Elegantly restored 1876 residence with six guest rooms.

EDITH PALMER'S COUNTRY INN, 775-847-7070, www.edithpalmers.com. Victorian-style accommodation in 19th-century homes.

THE B STREET HOUSE BED & BREAKFAST, 775-847-7231, www.BstreetHouse.com. Three-room inn in the authentically restored 1876 home of saloon and opera house entrepreneur Henry Piper.

THE GOLD HILL HOTEL, 775-847-7011, www.goldhillhotel.net. Twenty historic and new lodgings in Gold Hill.

Restaurants

CAFÉ DEL RIO, 775-847-5151. Locals' favorite for fine Southwestern cuisine.

DINNER AT THE CIDER FACTORY, 775-240-7665. Weekend dinners in the 19th-century cider house at Edith Palmer's Country Inn.

PALACE SALOON & RESTAURANT, 775-847-4441. Burgers, salads, and casual cuisine in a colorful saloon setting.

Winnemucca

For more information: Winnemucca Convention & Visitors Authority, 50 W. Winnemucca Blvd., 775-623-5071 or 800-962-2638 (toll-free within the USA), www.winnemucca.com.

Hotels

MOTEL SCOTT SHADY COURT, 775-623-3646. Comfortable retro-style motor court.

RED LION INN & CASINO, 775-623-2565 or 800-633-6435 (toll-free within the USA), www.redlionwinn.com. Contemporary motel and casino.

STONEHOUSE COUNTRY INN, 775-578-3530, www.stonehouse.freeservers.com. Bed-and-breakfast accommodation in Paradise Valley.

Restaurants

ORMACHEA'S DINNER HOUSE, 775-623-3455. Basque meals in an upscale setting.

PARTNERS IN WINE, 775-623-9000. A new take on Basque cuisine.

THE MARTIN HOTEL, 775-623-3197. Family-style Basque dining in a historic building.

NEW MEXICO

For more information: New Mexico Tourism Department, 491 Old Santa Fe Trail, Santa Fe, NM 87501, 800-733-6396 (toll-free within the USA), www.newmexico.org.

Acoma

Hotels

ACOMA SKY CITY CASINO HOTEL, 888-759-2489, www.skycity.com. Large modern resort and casino, close to Sky City Cultural Center and Acoma pueblo.

Chimayó, Las Trampas & Truchas

Hotels

CASA ESCONDIDA, 505-351-4805 or 800-643-7201 (toll-free within the USA), www.casaescondida.com. Eight guest rooms in a secluded bed-and-breakfast.

HACIENDA RANCHO DE CHIMAYO, 505-351-2222 or 888-270-2320 (toll-free within the USA), www.ranchodechimayo.com. Seven-room bed-and-breakfast arrayed around a courtyard in the hacienda of an old ranchito.

Restaurants

LEONA'S RESTAURANTE DE CHIMAYO, 505-351-4569. Tamales and other Mexican dishes in an informal restaurant adjacent to the Santuario.

RANCHO DE CHIMAYO, 505-351-4444. Fine New Mexican cuisine in a ranch house that dates back to the 1800s.

CORTINA TEA ROOM AND GALLERY, 505-689-1123. Coffee, tea, and light meals in an artist's studio in Truchas.

Cimarron & Raton

For more information: Cimarron Chamber of Commerce, 104 N. Lincoln Ave., P.O. Box 604, Cimarron, NM 87714, 505-376-2417, www.cimarronnm.com. Raton Chamber of Commerce, P.O. Box 1211, 100 Clayton Road, Raton, NM 87740, 800-638-6161 (toll-free within the USA), www.raton.info.

Hotels

CASA DEL GAVILAN, 575-376-2246, www.casadelgavilan.com. Boutique bed-and-breakfast in an adobe villa built in 1910 outside Cimarron.

EL PORTAL HOTEL, 505-445-3631 or 888-362-7345 (toll-free within the USA), www.elportalhotel.com. Comfortable, renovated rooms in a turn-of-the-century hotel in Raton.

ST. JAMES HOTEL, 505-376-2664 or 866-472-5019 (toll-free within the USA), www.stjamescimarron.com. Fourteen-room hotel that once welcomed Jesse James and Bat Masterson, in Cimarron's historic district.

Restaurants

COLFAX TAVERN, 505-376-2229. Quirky roadside tavern about 10 miles north of Cimarron.

ICE HOUSE RESTAURANT, 505-445-2339. Steaks and seafood in a rustic ice-storage building.

ST. JAMES HOTEL, 505-376-2664. Upscale dining in a historic hotel dining room in Cimarron.

Las Vegas

For more information: Las Vegas/San Miguel County Chamber of Commerce, P.O. Box 128, Las Vegas, NM 87701, 505-425-8631, www.lasvegasnewmexico.com.

Hotels

PLAZA HOTEL, 505-425-3591 or 800-328-1882 (toll-free within the USA), www.plazahotel-nm.com. Beautifully renovated 1882 hotel on the town plaza.

Restaurants

CHARLIE'S SPIC & SPAN BAKERY & CAFÉ, 505-426-1921. Easygoing diner that's a locals' favorite.

D'VINO'S, 505-425-3805. Italian cuisine in a historic block.

EL RIALTO, 505-454-0037. Mexican specialties in an expansive family-owned restaurant on Bridge St.

LANDMARK GRILL, 505-425-3591. Lively restaurant and bar in the historic Plaza Hotel.

Mesilla

For more information: Las Cruces Convention Visitor Bureau, 2121 N. Water St., Las Cruces, NM 88001, www.lascrucescvb.org. Town of Mesilla, P.O. Box 10, 2231 Avenida de Mesilla, Mesilla, NM 88046, 575-524-3262, www.mesilla-nm.org.

Hotels

MESON DE MESILLA, 575-525-9212 or 800-732-6025 (toll-free within the USA), www.mesondemesilla.com. Sophisticated boutique hotel close to the historic district.

Restaurants

DOUBLE EAGLE, 575-523-6700. New Mexico cuisine in an elaborately restored building that dates to the 1840s.

LA POSTA, 575-524-3524. Steaks and Mexican dishes in an atmospheric mid-19th-century Territorial-style compound.

THE TORCH, 575-525-9212. Gourmet contemporary Southwestern meals in a jazz-club setting.

Taos

For more information: Taos County Chamber of Commerce, P. O. Drawer 1, Taos, NM 87571 or 800-732-8267 (toll-free within the USA), www.taoschamber.com. Taos Pueblo, P.O. Box 1856, Taos, NM 87571, 575-758-1028, www.taospueblo.com.

Hotels

DON FERNANDO DE TAOS, 575-758-4444 or 800-759-2736 (toll-free within the USA), www.donfernandodetaos.com. Comfortable, spacious motel-style rooms 2 miles south of the plaza.

HISTORIC TAOS INN, 575-758-2233 or 888-519-8267 (toll-free within the USA), www.taosinn.com. Renovated inn incorporating the century-old home of Taos's first doctor.

HOTEL LA FONDA DE TAOS, 575-758-2211 or 800-833-2211 (toll-free within the USA), www.lafondataos.com. Upscale contemporary Southwest accommodation on the plaza.

MABEL DODGE LUHAN HOUSE, 575-751-9686 or 800-846-2235 (toll-free within the USA), www.mabeldodgeluhan.com. Twenty-two-room bed-and-breakfast an the adobe house built in 1918 by a noted patron of the arts.

Restaurants

DOC MARTIN'S RESTAURANT AND ADOBE BAR, 575-758-1977. Creative Southwestern cuisine in a historic hotel and local gathering place.

DOWNTOWN BISTRO, 575-737-5060. Sophisticated wine bar and meals.

ESKE'S BREW PUB, 575-758-1517. Handcrafted beers and light meals in a lively pub.

JOSEPH'S TABLE, 575-751-4512. Elegant gourmet meals in the Hotel La Fonda de Taos.

MICHAEL'S KITCHEN, 575-758-4178. Pastries and breakfast in a lively casual restaurant.

ORLANDO'S NEW MEXICAN CAFÉ, 575-751-1450. Locals' favorite for Southwestern dishes in a colorful cottage.

STAKEOUT GRILL & BAR, 575-758-2042. Steaks in a country setting with fantastic views.

TRADING POST CAFÉ, 505-758-5089. Fine Mediterranean cuisine in Ranchos de Taos.

UTAH

For more information: Utah Office of Tourism, Council Hall/Capital Hill, 300 North State Street, Salt Lake City, UT 84114, 800-200-1160 (toll-free within the USA), www.utah.travel.

Bluff

For more information: San Juan County, 117 S. Main Street, P.O. Box 490, Monticello, UT 84535, 435-587-3235 or 800-574-4386 (toll-free within the USA), www.utahscanyoncountry.com.

Hotels

CALF CANYON B & B, 435-672-2470 or 888-922-2470 (toll-free within the USA), www.calfcanyon.com. Bed-and-breakfast in a new pioneer-style home in the historic district.

DECKER HOUSE INN, 435-672-2304 or 888-637-2582 (toll-free within the USA), www.deckerhouseinn.com. Bed-and-breakfast accommodation in a historic house from 1898.

DESERT ROSE INN & CABINS, 435-672-2303 or 888-475-7673 (toll-free within the USA), www.Desertroseinn.com. Comfortable new lodge with spacious rooms.

GOULDINGS MONUMENT VALLEY TRADING POST AND LODGE, 435-727-3231, www.gouldings.com. Historic trading post and lodge with modern rooms, at the edge of Monument Valley on the Utah–Arizona border.

Restaurants

TWIN ROCKS CAFÉ, 435-672-2341. Regional cuisine in a trading post dining room in the shadow of the Twin Rocks formation.

COTTONWOOD STEAKHOUSE, 435-672-2282. Western-style barbecue with outdoor seating.

COW CANYON RESTAURANT, 435-672-2208. Well-prepared Southwestern dishes in a restaurant attached to a trading post and gallery.

Escalante & Boulder

For more information: Garfield County Office of Tourism, P.O. Box 200, 55 South Main Street, Panguitch, UT 84759, 800-444-6689, www.brycecanyoncountry.com; Escalante Chamber of Commerce, P.O. Box 175, Escalante, UT 84726, 435-826-4810, www.escalante-cc.com; Boulder Business Group, www.boulderutah.com.

Hotels

BOULDER MOUNTAIN LODGE, 435-335-7460 or 800-556-3446 (toll-free within the USA), www.boulder-utah.com/lodge.html. Luxurious Western-style eco-lodge overlooking a small bird sanctuary.

PROSPECTOR INN, 435-826-4653, www.prospectorinn.com. Modern 50-room motel near the entrance to Grand Staircase Escalante National Monument.

Restaurants

BOULDER MESA RESTAURANT, 435-335-7447. Casual dining in the heart of Boulder.

BRYCE CANYON PINES, 435-834-5441. Longtime locals' favorite on Scenic Hwy 12, in the Bryce Canyon area.

COWBOY BLUES RESTAURANT, 435-826-4577. Well-prepared dishes in a casual art-filled setting in Escalante.

GOLDEN LOOP CAFÉ, 435-826-4433. Hearty breakfasts on Escalante's Main Street.

HELL'S BACKBONE GRILL, 435-335-7464. Casually elegant restaurant in Boulder, with an imaginative menu focusing on organic regional cuisine.

Kanab

For more information: Kane County Office of Tourism and Film Commission, P.O. Box 209, Kanab, UT 84741, 435-644-5033 or 800-733-5263 (toll-free within the USA), www.kaneutah.com.

Hotels

PARRY LODGE, 435-644-2601 or 800-748-4104 (toll-free within the USA), www.parrylodge.com. Comfortable motel accommodation in a lodge with ties to the Western movie industry.

THE AVOCA HOUSE, 435-644-3172; www.theavocahouse.com. Bed-and-breakfast inn located in a house built in 1912 from a Sears, Roebuck & Co. kit.

Restaurants

ESCOBAR'S MEXICAN RESTAURANT, 435-644-3739. Established family-owned restaurant with south-of-the-border dishes.

HOUSTON'S TRAIL'S END RESTAURANT, 435-644-2488. Char-broiled steaks and seafood served amid Western decor.

REWIND DINER, 435-644-3200. Retro-style diner highlighting Mediterranean dishes and American comfort food.

ROCKING V CAFÉ, 435-644-8001. Eclectic "slow-food" menu in Kanab's original mercantile building, built in 1892.

Manti, Spring City & Ephraim

For more information: Sanpete Travel & Economic Development, P.O. Box 148, 191 North Main St., Manti, UT 84642, 435-835-6877 or 800-2818-4346 (toll-free within the USA), www.sanpete.com.

Hotels

MANTI HOUSE INN, 435-835-0161 or 800-835-7512 (toll-free within the USA), www.mantihouseinn.com. Bed-and-breakfast inn in a historic 1880s house across from the Manti Utah Temple.

OSBORNE HOUSE, 435-462-9338, or 877-462-1894 (toll-free within the USA), www.osborneinn.com. Four-room bed-and-breakfast in a renovated 1894 Victorian home in the center of Spring City.

SPRING CITY INN & ANTIQUES, 435-602-9787, www.springcityinn.com. Newly renovated 1880s stone house with five guest rooms on Main Street in Spring City.

WILLOW CREEK INN, 435-283-4566, www.hotelwillowcreekinn.com. Modern and comfortable motel accommodation centrally located in Ephraim.

Restaurants

MANTI HOUSE INN, 435-835-0161. Locals' favorite for family occasions in a historic house.

ROY'S PIZZA/TIN PLATE PASTA, 435-283-4222. Pizza and adjoining pasta kitchen in a retro-style dining room on the first floor of the former Ephraim Hotel.

SPRING CITY KITCHEN, 435-462-9822. Breakfast and lunch in a community gathering place on Main Street.

Moab

For more information: Moab Area Travel Council, P.O. Box 550, Moab, Utah 84532, 435-259-8825 or 800-635-6622 (toll-free within the USA), www.discovermoab.com.

Hotels

BEST WESTERN CANYONLANDS, 435-259-2300 or 800-649-5191 (toll-free within the USA), www.canyonlandsinn.com. Modern motel with spacious rooms in the center of Moab.

GONZO INN, 435-259-2515 or 800-791-4044 (toll-free within the USA), www.gonzoinn.com. Southwestern inn with hip retro decor.

RED CLIFFS LODGE, 435-259-2002, or 866-812-2002 (toll-free within the USA), www.redcliffslodge.com. Riverfront cabins and lodge, with an onsite winery, 16 miles beyond town, on the Colorado River.

SORREL RIVER RANCH, 435-259-4642, or 877-359-2715 (toll-free within the USA), www.sorrelriver.com. Deluxe western resort 17 miles outside Moab on the banks of the Colorado River.

Restaurants

CENTER CAFÉ, 435-259-4295. Dishes highlighting seasonal and organic ingredients served in a casually elegant dining room.

DESERT BISTRO, 435-259-0756. Gourmet contemporary Southwestern cuisine in a historic ranch house.

JAILHOUSE CAFÉ, 435-259-3900. Locals' favorite breakfast place in the old courthouse and jail.

LA HACIENDA, 435-259-6319. Long-established family-owned Mexican restaurant.

SINGHA, 435-259-0039. Authentic Thai cuisine in a well-appointed setting.

Park City

For more information: Park City Chamber of Commerce/Convention and Visitors Bureau, P.O. Box 1630, 1910 Prospector Ave., Park City, UT 84060, 435-649-6100 or 800-453-1360 (toll-free within the USA), www.parkcityinfo.com.

Hotels

SKY LODGE, 435-6588-2500 or 888-876-2525 (toll-free within the USA), www.theskylodge.com. Stylish, contemporary luxury hotel, with 33 1-, 2-, and 3-bedroom suites, at the edge of Main Street in Park City.

STEIN ERIKSEN LODGE, 435-649-3700 or 800-435-1302 (toll-free within the USA), www.steinlodge.com. Deluxe Old World-style lodge next to the ski slopes in Deer Valley.

WASHINGTON SCHOOL INN, 435-649-3800 or 800-824-1672 (toll-free within the USA), www.washingtonschoolinn.com. Historic 1889 schoolhouse superbly renovated as an upscale 15-room bed-and-breakfast.

Restaurants

GRAPPA, 435-645-0636. Northern Italian cuisine in a turn-of-the-century building that was once a miners' boarding house.

NO NAME SALOON AND GRILL, 435-649-6667. Sandwiches and burgers in a locals' hangout.

PURPLE SAGE, 435-655-9505. Southwestern dishes in a historic Main Street setting.

ROYAL STREET CAFÉ, 435-645-6724. Eclectic menu at scenic Silver Lake Lodge in Deer Valley.

SHABU, 435-645-7253. Innovative Asian tapas and shabu-shabu, prepared at the table.

THE RIVERHORSE ON MAIN, 435-649-3536. Fine American contemporary cuisine.

WAHSO, 435-615-0300. Elegant dining with Pan-Asian flavors.

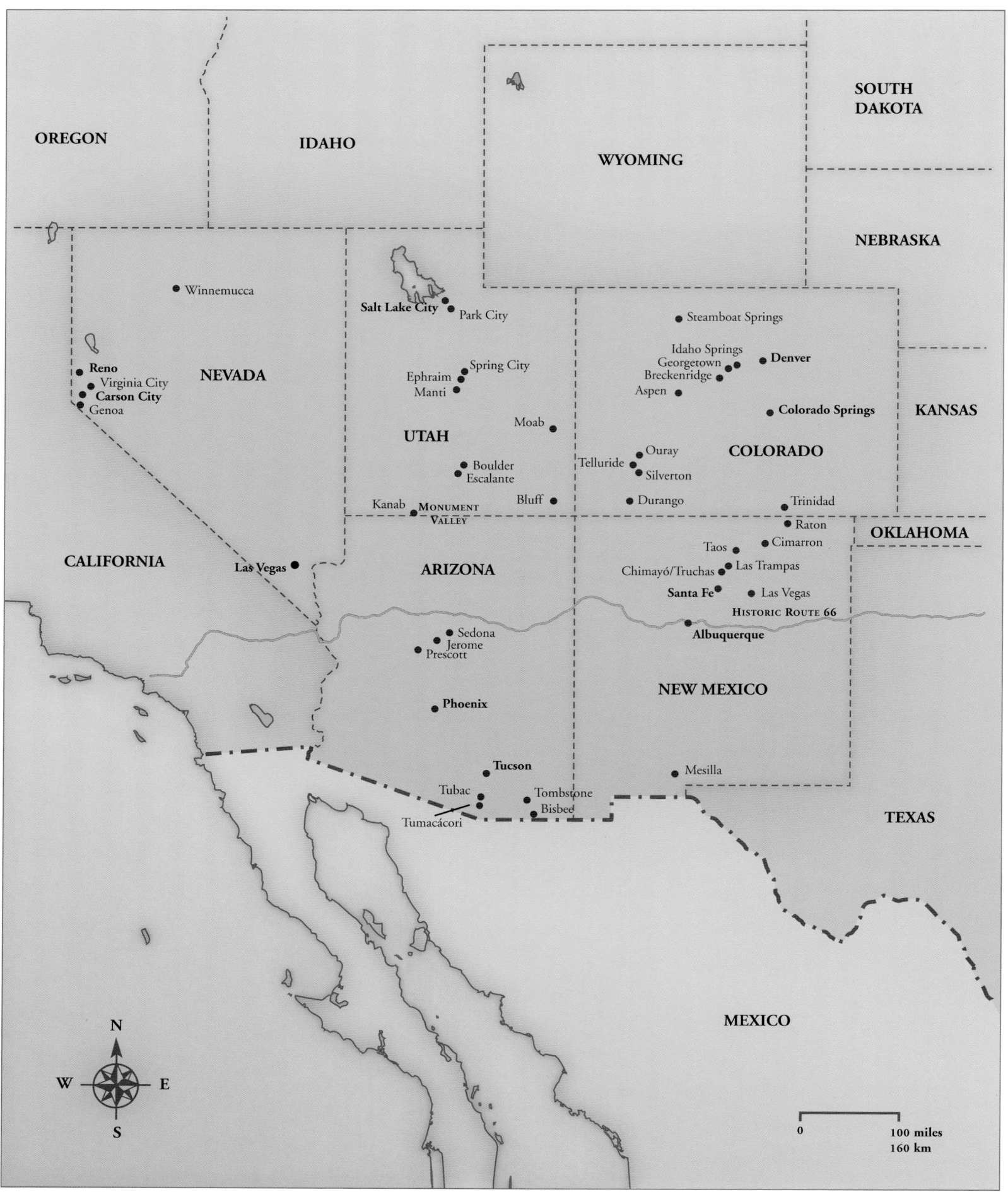

OREGON

IDAHO

WYOMING

SOUTH
DAKOTA

NEBRASKA

NEVADA

● Winnemucca

Salt Lake City ● Park City

● Steamboat Springs

Idaho Springs
Georgetown
Breckenridge ● **Denver**
Aspen ●

Reno
Virginia City
Carson City
Genoa

Spring City
Ephraim
Manti

Moab

UTAH

Colorado Springs

KANSAS

COLORADO

Boulder
Escalante

Telluride ● Ouray
Silverton

Kanab ● **MONUMENT
VALLEY**

Bluff

Durango

Trinidad

Raton

CALIFORNIA

● **Las Vegas**

ARIZONA

Taos ● Cimarron OKLAHOMA

Chimayó/Truchas ● Las Trampas
Santa Fe ● ● Las Vegas

HISTORIC ROUTE 66

Sedona
Jerome
Prescott

Albuquerque

NEW MEXICO

● **Phoenix**

Tucson

Tubac

● Mesilla

Tombstone
Bisbee

TEXAS

Tumacácori

MEXICO

N

W ● E

S

0   100 miles
160 km

Selected Reading

The following books provide interesting background for the chapters and essays in this book.

History, natural history, culture, and essays:
Abbey, Edward, *Desert Solitaire* (1968)
Dary, David, *The Santa Fe Trail: Its History, Legends, and Lore* (2000)
Dedek, Peter, *Hip to the Trip: A Cultural History of Route 66* (2007)
Robotham, Tom, *Ghost Towns: How They Were Born, How They Lived, and How They Died* (1993)
Rochlin, Harriet, and Fred Rochlin, *Pioneer Jews: A New Life in the Far West* (2000)
Shoumatoff, Alex, *Legends of the American Desert: Sojourns in the Greater Southwest* (1997)
Sprague, Marshall, *Colorado, A History* (1984)
Stegner, Wallace, *Mormon Country* (1942, paperback 2003)
Thybony, Scott, *Burntwater* (1997)
Till, Tom, and Teresa Jordan, *Great Ghost Towns of the West* (2001)
Trumble, Marshall, *Arizona: A Cavalcade of History* (1989)
Udall, Stewart L., *Majestic Journey: Coronado's Inland Empire* (1995)
Wallis, Michael, *Route 66: The Mother Road* (1990)
Ward, Geoffrey C., *The West: An Illustrated History* (1996)
Zwinger, Anne, *Wind in the Rock* (1978)

Native American history and culture:
Noble, David Grant, *Ancient Ruins of the Southwest: An Archaeological Guide* (2000)
Page, Jake, *In the Hands of the Great Spirit: The 20,000-Year History of American Indians* (2003)
Page, Suzanne, and Jake Page, *Field Guide to Southwest Indian Arts and Crafts* (1998)
Plog, Stephen, *Ancient Peoples of the American Southwest* (1997)
Trimble, Stephen, *The People: Indians of the American Southwest* (1993)

Individual towns, local histories, memoirs, and biographies:
Backus, Harriet Fish, *Tomboy Bride* (1980)
DeQuille, Dan, *The Big Bonanza* (1876, reprinted 1980)
Hillerman, Tony, *The Great Taos Bank Robbery* (1973)
James, Ronald M., *The Roar and the Silence: A History of Virginia City and the Comstock Lode* (1998)
Luhan, Mabel Dodge, *Winter in Taos* (1935, paperback 2007)
Royem, Robert T., *America's Railroad: The Official Guidebook of the Durango & Silverton Narrow Gauge Railroad* (2007)
Ruland-Thorne, Kate, *Sedona: Legends and Legacies* (1989)
Smith, Duane A., *Rocky Mountain Boom Town: A History of Durango* (1980)
Smith, P. David, *A Quick History of Ouray* (1996)
Taylor, Don, *The United States of America v. the "Cowboys"* (2006)
Tefertiller, Casey, *Wyatt Earp: The Life Behind the Legend* (1997)
Twain, Mark, *Roughing It* (originally published 1872)
Warren, Larry, *Park City: Mountain of Treasure* (2004)

Fiction:
Cather, Willa, *Death Comes for the Archbishop* (originally published in 1927)
Hillerman, Tony, *A Thief of Time* (1988)
Nichols, John, *The Milagro Beanfield War* (1974)

Acknowledgments

The author and photographer are grateful to the following individuals and organizations for their help in researching this book:

INDIVIDUALS
Chris Chrystal
Rich Frank
Marcus Gottschalk
Malcolm Griffiths
Cosette Henritze
Bonnie and Jock Jones
Ken Knapp
Michael London
Erik Thompson
Larry Warren

ARIZONA
Arizona Office of Tourism
Bisbee
Bisbee Convention and Visitors' Bureau
Copper Queen Courtyard Hotel
Shady Dell
Queen Mine Tour
Canyon de Chelly
Holiday Inn
Flagstaff
Flagstaff Convention and Visitors' Bureau
Inn Suites
Jerome
Connor Hotel of Jerome
Prescott
Prescott Area Coalition for Tourism
Prescott Chamber of Commerce
Hassayampa Inn
Hotel Vendome
Log Cabin Bed & Breakfast
Sedona
Sedona Chamber of Commerce Tourism
   Bureau
Enchantment Resort and Mii Amo
Pink Jeep Tours
Sheila Donnelly & Associates
Tombstone
Cochise County, Arizona
Tombstone Chamber of Commerce
Larian Motel
Tubac & Tumacácori
Tubac Chamber of Commerce
Tubac Golf Resort

COLORADO
Colorado Tourism Office
Aspen
Aspen Chamber Resort Association

Aspen Historical Society
Mountain Chalet
The Little Nell
Breckenridge
Breckenridge Resort Chamber
Breckenridge Heritage Alliance
Great Divide Lodge
Mountain Thunder Lodge
Durango & Silverton
Durango Area Tourism Office
Silverton Chamber of Commerce
General Palmer Hotel
Rochester Hotel/The Leland House
Villa Dellavalle Inn
The Old Hundred Mine
Georgetown & Idaho Springs
Historic Georgetown, Inc.
All Aboard Inn
Georgetown Loop Historic Mining &
   Railroad Park
Ouray
Ouray Chamber Resort Association
Beaumont Hotel
Box Canyon Lodge
Bachelor Syracuse Mine Tour
Steamboat Springs
Steamboat Springs Chamber Resort
   Association
Mountain Resorts
Sheraton Steamboat Hotel
Telluride
Telluride Tourism Board
Mountain Lodge
Resort Quest

NEVADA
Nevada Commission on Tourism
Genoa
David Walley's Resort
The Wild Rose Inn
Virginia City
Virginia City Convention & Tourism
   Authority
B Street House Bed & Breakfast
Edith Palmer's Country Inn
Winnemucca
Winnemucca Convention & Visitors
   Authority
Red Lion Inn and Casino
Scott's Shady Court

NEW MEXICO
New Mexico Tourism Department
Acoma
Sky City Cultural Center & Casino Hotel
Chimayó
Hacienda Rancho de Chimayo
Cimarron & Raton
El Portal Hotel
Casa del Gavilan
Las Vegas
Plaza Hotel
Mesilla
Las Cruces Convention Visitor Bureau
Meson de Mesilla
Taos
Taos County Chamber of Commerce
Taos Pueblo
Don Fernando de Taos
Historic Taos Inn

UTAH
Utah Office of Tourism
Bluff
San Juan County Economic Development
   and Visitor Services
Desert Rose Inn & Cabins
Gouldings Monument Valley Trading Post
   and Lodge
Wild Rivers Expeditions
Escalante & Boulder
Garfield County Travel Council
Boulder Mountain Lodge
Prospector Inn
Kanab
Kane County Office of Tourism & Film
   Commission
Parry Lodge
Dreamland Safari Tours
Manti, Spring City, & Ephraim
Sanpete County Office of Economic
   Development
Moab
Moab Area Travel Council
Best Western Canyonlands Inn
Moab Adventure Center
Park City
Park City Chamber of
   Commerce/Convention & Visitors Bureau
Washington School Inn